THE WAY OF ST JAMES
A CYCLISTS' GUIDE

About the Author

John Higginson has been a long-distance fell walker for many years. Having been a keen cyclist in his youth, he took up cycling again a few years ago after retiring from the post of headmaster at a Cheshire primary school. He is now a professional writer and lecturer.

He and his wife, Andrea, spent two years researching the pilgrimage before embarking on their first journey to Santiago de Compostela in 1997, and they have spent much of their time riding alternative routes ever since. They now live in France, only a few kilometres from the pilgrim route, and are both active members of the Confraternity of Saint James. Before making the journey in 2004 they had ridden on two of the other pilgrimage routes, that from Vezelay and also a part of the Arles route.

Other Cicerone guides by the author

Cycling in the Loire – The Way of Saint Martin
The Danube Cycleway – Donaueschingen to Budapest

THE WAY OF SAINT JAMES

A CYCLISTS' GUIDE
from Le Puy en Velay to Santiago de Compostela

by
John Higginson

2 POLICE SQUARE, MILNTHORPE, CUMBRIA LA7 7PY
www.cicerone.co.uk

© John Higginson 1999, 2005
ISBN-10: 1 85284 441 8
ISBN-13: 978 1 85284 441 7

First edition 1999
Second edition 2005
Reprinted 2009, 2012 and 2016 (with updates)

Printed by KHL Printing, Singapore
A catalogue record for this book is available from the British Library.
Photographs by Andrea Higginson

Dedication

In memory of my father, a quiet adventurer.

Acknowledgements

With thanks to the people of the camino, whose cheerful support is the
lifeblood of the pilgrimage, and also to 'Sur les Chemins de Compostelle',
based in Cahors, for all their support over the past ten years.
May the true spirit of pilgrimage overcome the falsehood of
commercialism, which is a real threat to its future.

Updates to this Guide

While every effort is made by our authors to ensure the accuracy of guide-
books as they go to print, changes can occur during the lifetime of an edition. Any updates that we know of for this guide will be on the Cicerone
website (**www.cicerone.co.uk/441/updates**), so please check before planning your trip. We also advise that you check information about such things
as transport, accommodation and shops locally. Even rights of way can be
altered over time.

We are always grateful for information about any discrepancies between
a guidebook and the facts on the ground, sent by email to info@cicerone.
co.uk or by post to Cicerone, 2 Police Square, Milnthorpe LA7 7PY, United
Kingdom.

Front cover: Chapel of St. Roch – snow in May! (Stage 2)

CONTENTS

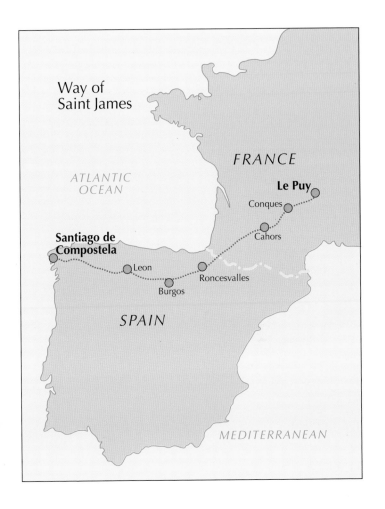

Map Key

AutoRoute/Autoria	————————
Main road	————————
Minor road	————————
Route on main road	▪▪▪▪▪▪▪▪▪▪▪▪▪▪
Route on minor road	··············
Route on country lane	••••••••••••••
River	〜〜〜
Lake/sea	⬭
Town/village	⬮
Forest	▨

PREFACE TO THE THIRD EDITION

The most significant change since 2004 is the almost universal use of the internet for information and research, but the route and destination remain the same. Owing to the popularity and publicity of the route many more accommodations have opened, likewise assisted transport from major points. It is sadly more advisable, therefore, to book accommodation in advance, thus eliminating some of the sense of adventure.

John Higginson

PREFACE TO THE SECOND EDITION

Researched and written during holy year 2004 (a holy year is when St James' Day, 25 July, falls on a Sunday), this new edition of *The Way of Saint James – A Cyclists' Guide* attempts to take into account all the changes that have affected pilgrims on the way to Santiago de Compostela in the seven years since the first edition was researched in July and August 1997. As new roads (especially in northern Spain) and accommodation are appearing all the time – and others closing – revision was obviously needed, and this new edition should now prove reliable for several years to come.

Many thousands of people follow the pilgrim route to Santiago de Compstela each year, and as a consequence the route that is laid out and waymarked is extremely worn and not navigable for touring cyclists. In 1997, as touring cyclists who would never see 50 again, my wife and I realised that if we were to attain our goal of cycling from Le Puy to Santiago, we would have to devise our own route – one which followed as closely as possible the original pilgrim way, visiting all the important sites along it, yet avoiding the actual camino unless it followed the tarmac. This book is the result of our efforts. It is neither perfect nor definitive, but simply our way of achieving our goal by sitting and pedalling, rather than pushing, our bikes along the Way of St. James.

This is very much a pilgrim's guide rather than a touring cyclist's schedule. My wife and I are not racing cyclists, nor even hardy long-distance riders, and we found that on most days 50–80km was our limit. The average distance travelled per day on each stage in this book is about 50km – easily within the compass of the moderately fit who are interested in using the bicycle as the most efficient means of making the pilgrimage to Santiago de Compostela.

John Higginson

Santiago de Compostela cathedral

INTRODUCTION

In the past ten years many books and guides have been written about the pilgrimage to Santiago de Compostela. They are all based on a route which, with a few variations each year to circumnavigate building work, roadworks and worn-out pathways, has been clearly waymarked and laid out as close as possible to the original pilgrim way. This route is now travelled by thousands of pilgrims each year, constantly making it deeper and wider, with the result that non-walkers also tend to find themselves on the pathway. Horse riders manage quite well, but cyclists have a number of problems. Those on mountain bikes are able to bounce their way over the boulders and ruts which are to be found everywhere, but risk the abuse of walkers who feel (quite justifiably) that their territory is being encroached upon, whereas touring cyclists find much of the track impossible to negotiate and so must look for alternatives, which are offered in this book.

Using roads with a good surface for touring cyclists, this guide sets out to follow the original pilgrimage route (camino) as closely as possible. It offers the opportunity to visit every major church and shrine along the way, and includes a few detours to outlying monasteries for good measure. Several variants are also given,

to provide for the fit and not-so-fit pilgrim, and accommodation along the way in gîtes d'étape (the French equivalent of a superior youth hostel), chambres d'hôte (similar to English bed and breakfast), hotels, refugios (Spanish refuges) and hostals (small hotels, also called fondas and hospedaje) is listed. For those who want something extra, routes from Santiago to Finisterre and to Padrón are also included (Appendixes 1 and 2).

The route has been divided into easy daily stages, some of which are

Pilgrim statue in Sahagún (Stage 19/20)

Les Estrets – landslide (Stage 2)

shorter than others, to accommodate time taken crossing mountain ranges, or riding on difficult roads, or because of fascinating places to visit. It is not prescriptive, however, and those with stronger legs and more courage may wish to split the journey differently. Some sections of the route are devoid of accommodation, and these stages are longer than they should be. If new hotels or hostels are opened in the future, then the lengths of these stages could easily be rethought.

The roads used are almost always surfaced with tarmac. In France they tend to be quiet country lanes, and even the short stretches of Routes Nationals are of good quality and not busy. French drivers often sound their horns to warn you of their approach, and give you a wide berth and a cheery wave as they pass. In Spain

there are few country lanes. Most of the roads are wide and fast, and they usually have a narrow hard shoulder which doubles as a cycle lane. Drivers do not tend to give cyclists much room, and heavy lorries often streak down these roads with their nearside wheel straddling the hard shoulder. However, compared with English roads we found most Spanish ones to be very quiet.

In general, road surfaces were as good as those found in England, but main streets in villages and small towns, particularly in Spain, are often cobbled, with deep drains running down the centre. Negotiate them with care, especially in wet weather when they become very slippery. Expect to find farm animals wandering at will on Spanish country roads and in villages, and expect to find dogs everywhere.

HISTORY

Saint James

James the Great, Jesus' cousin and brother of St John, is as much a character of legend in Spain as St George is in England. Facts about his life are hard to come by, although it is fairly certain that he was beheaded by Herod Agrippa in Jerusalem in 44AD, making him the first disciple to be martyred. The rest, however, is mere hypothesis. Reference is made in a Greek text to James having visited Spain on an evangelising mission, but if it did occur its success was strictly limited. It is believed that James then returned to the Holy Land, where he met his fate. But it is after his death that James' legend takes wings of fantasy.

His body and head are said to have been taken by his followers, Athanasius and Theodoro, to Jaffa where a stone boat (literally, a boat made from stone, according to the legend) was commissioned. Within a week this boat and its precious cargo were washed up at Iria Flavia (modern day Padrón), only 20km from present-day Santiago de Compostela. Athanasius and Theodoro were at first imprisoned, then released as a result of angelic intervention, and eventually James was buried.

For 800 years he appears to have lain undisturbed and forgotten, until a hermit called Pelagius had a vision of a star shining on a field. Again, legend has it that this resulted in the discovery of the tombs of St James and his companions. It was not long before Alfonso II, King of the Asturias, declared St James patron saint of Spain, and soon visions of *Santiago Matamoros* (Saint James the Moor-slayer) were being seen during battles against the Moorish invader, most notably at the Battle of Clavijo, where he is said to have appeared on a white charger to lead the Spanish troops. A church and monastery were built over the tombs and so the history of Santiago de Compostela began.

The name Santiago de Compostela either originated from *campus stellae*, meaning field of stars, referring to the place of the tombs' discovery, or from the Latin componere, indicating

Santiago de Compostela – St James welcomes pilgrims

13

O Cebreiro – view from the village (Stage 24/25)

a Roman necropolis. In an interesting recent discovery, the interior of one of the tombs has been found to bear an inscription in Greek: 'Athanasius martyr'.

Pilgrimage

In the past, people went on pilgrimage for a wide variety of reasons, many of which were personal – pilgrims might want to atone for their sins, for example, or to profess their faith. Some, rather like today's tourists, wanted to visit shrines and venerate holy relics, and some were even there on behalf of rich clients who were too busy to go for themselves. But many pilgrims began their journey, at least, simply to escape the drudgery of their medieval lives.

The appeal of Santiago de Compostela was manifold. After its capture in 1078 by the Turks, the Holy Sepulchre in Jerusalem had become

14

almost impossible to visit, and for many a pilgrimage to Rome to see the tomb of St Peter meant a crossing of the Alps with all its attendant hazards. However, the journey to Santiago had much to recommend it: it was a good long way to travel, it had enough difficulties to make it arduous but not impossible, and it had a wealth of shrines and relics to visit on the way. Also, it was heavily promoted by both Spain and the French church at Cluny, who saw it as not only a source of future wealth, but also a way of resisting the threat of Moorish dominance.

As the popularity of the pilgrimage to Santiago de Compostela grew (over half a million people per year in the 11th century), so the number of monasteries, hospitals and hermitages to assist the pilgrims along the way also burgeoned. In the middle of the 12th century, Aimery Picaud, a monk from central France, produced the first ever guide to the pilgrimage, as part of his *Codex Calixtinus*. Picaud included not only descriptions of the holy sites, but also his own unrestrained views on the character and customs of the inhabitants of the regions through which the pilgrim would pass.

The pilgrim way to Santiago retained its popularity until the end of the 15th century, and indeed never fully declined. But thanks in no small part to the efforts this century of the priest of the village of O Cebreiro, Dr Elias Valiña Sampedro, the pilgrimage is now enjoying a great resurgence. If its popularity continues to grow, especially during holy years (when St James' Day, 25 July, falls on a Sunday), then Santiago may no longer be able to cope with the enormous number of visitors who will descend on it, not just from along the pilgrimage routes, but also by air, road and rail.

It is probable that one of the very first pilgrims from Le Puy, Bishop Gottschalk, rode on a horse to Santiago, as did the intrepid Aimery Picaud. Cycling pilgrims, therefore, should not feel inferior to their walking counterparts. They are simply using the mode of transport most suitable for them. There is something of a hierarchy amongst the pilgrims along the way – walkers look down on cyclists, those who do the whole route look down on those who only cover part of it, those who make the journey under their own steam look down on those who travel its length by car, and everyone looks down on the daytrippers who wander around Santiago with their broomstick staffs and plastic water-gourds – but this attitude should really be discouraged. We are all pilgrims and should be allowed to make our own pilgrimage in our own way.

PREPARATION

Bicycles

We received a great deal of advice about the bikes we should take on this journey. Many traditionalists told us that the only machine they would entertain was a lightweight tourer, while others with a more modern outlook said that nothing but a mountain bike would cope with the terrain we would encounter. In the end the advice we took was sound and we were never to regret it – we chose American trail bikes with the strength of a mountain bike and the lightweight versatility of a tourer. They

Le Puy – Place du Plot (Stage 1)

Rabanal del Camino – English refuge (Stage 22)

were equipped with gears (42/32/22 drivetrain and 7-speed 11–28) low enough to cope, fully laden, with 1-in-4 hills, highly efficient brakes for the long, vertiginous descents, 'bulletproof' Kevlar tyres which did not puncture once in 1500km on either the first or second pilgrimage to Santiago, topped off with our own gel saddles for extra comfort. Our only mishap occurred the first time we cycled the route, when a broken spoke was sustained on the cobbles in a mountain village during a particularly steep descent, and thankfully we were carrying spare spokes (which are absolutely essential, as those available on mainland Europe are a different size from English ones).

Equipment

The first time we did this journey we were leaving from England, and as we expected to be away for anything up

to two months, we knew we had to be completely self sufficient during this time. We also knew that we had to keep the weight on the bikes down to a manageable amount, so we began by making a long list of 'essentials', and then removing from it anything that was not absolutely essential. The result was that on the first pilgrimage we took only one item we did not use, and on the second, none at all. ('If you are not going to use it every day, don't take it' is a good guide, although it doesn't apply to emergency equipment and weatherproof clothing.)

When it came to bags there was only one sensible choice – Ortlieb Bags (see Appendix 5). This was the only manufacturer we found who guarantees their products totally waterproof, and what a difference it makes. Even in torrential thunderstorms and driving sleet and snow, everything inside our panniers and bar bags stayed completely dry without having to be wrapped in polythene bags. Even the rubberised map case atop the bar bag kept out every drop of water – although it did turn yellow in the sun of the high plateau of the Meseta in Spain!

We did not take a tent and we did not regret it. The extra weight, and the effort to erect it at the end of a hard day and then strike camp early each morning when the fabric is often wet with dew, is just too much on a journey such as this, and the cost of a campsite is very similar to that of a gîte d'étape. The only items we took and did not use were self-inflating sleeping mats. They would have been useful if we had been allowed to stay in *refugios* (Spanish refuges), but they are certainly not essential. (See Appendix 3 for a full kit list.)

We had been warned about wild, dangerous dogs along the whole length of the pilgrimage route, so took a Dog-Dazer – a small, battery-powered device which emits a high-frequency sound that deters dogs from attacking. We have used it several times and it has not failed us yet (although we are told it does not work if the dog is deaf!). (See Appendix 5 for addresses.)

Maps and Guides

We tried to keep these to the minimum because paper weighs so much, but ended up taking IGN map numbers 50, 57, 58, 63 and 66 for France, and Michelin regional map

numbers 573, 575 and 571 for Spain. As soon as we had finished with each, we sent it home to reduce the weight. The IGN maps were excellent, with only one inaccuracy found, and they covered all but a few kilometres of the journey across France. The Michelins were not so good. The scale was not fine enough to show unnumbered roads, with some new roads missing, and those that were on the map often had different numbers from those we saw on the roads as we travelled. The only guides we took were the first edition of this book and the 2004 *Camino Francés Guide* (also called *The Pilgrim Guide to Spain*, from the Confraternity of St James). We had, however, read numerous books

Triacastela – camino waymarker

and guides before we left home and a list of these can be found in the bibliography in Appendix 6.

Accommodation

Most of our nights on the French portion of the way, with a couple of notable exceptions, were spent in some form of *gîte d'étape*. These had high minimum standards, including the provision of a decent bed, showers and a kitchen. These standards were more often than not exceeded, however, with private rooms, baths, washing machines, fridge-freezers and microwaves. In 2015 the price varied between 12 and 20 euros per person in hostels and *gîte d'étapes* and more in the *chambres d'hôtes* which are springing up along the route in France. In Spain, however, the story was very different. In the high season most *refugios* (up to 10 euros per person) refused entry to pilgrims on bikes

until after 8.00 p.m. because the beds were allocated to walkers who took precedence. In these circumstances we found alternative accommodation in small hotels (often called *hostals* or *fondas* or *hospedaje*), convents or monasteries. These were fine, but stretched our budget to its limit, costing us 35–50 euros per room (in 2004) – so be warned! Information about overnight stops is included for each section of the route, but reservations should be confirmed by telephone, as situations can change rapidly, especially in Spain.

Fitness

We had been planning our pilgrimage for two years and were determined to be fit for it. During the winter months we walked four to six miles every day, and in better weather we cycled on three or four days of the week, gradually increasing the distance

Montes de León – the route ahead (Stage 21)

and weight carried. No amount of cycling in Britain, however, can prepare anyone for the mountains they are going to meet on the route. It is not the steepness of the hills that is a shock, but the length. It is not unusual for a single hill to be 25km in length, with 32km the longest. Be prepared to spend four hours climbing one major peak. It happened several times. Tiredness can be cumulative, and getting on a bike every morning for four or five weeks and cycling all day in extreme weather conditions is very different from having a hard day out once a week in England.

Help Available

Before you leave on this pilgrimage, the best help you can have is from people who have been before. The simplest way to contact these people is through the Confraternity of St James (see Appendix 5, Useful Addresses), which exists to promote the pilgrimage and help future pilgrims. Do not be afraid to ask what may seem obvious and apparently stupid questions – if you do not ask, you will never gain essential information. Attendance at a 'Practical Pilgrim Seminar' run by the Confraternity would certainly be of great use. At the time of writing there are to be five seminars in the year, on five different dates, at locations in England, Wales and Scotland.

A pilgrim passport or *credencial* should be carried by all pilgrims. It consists of a book of blank spaces onto which dated stamps are printed. These stamps may be obtained at bars, churches, hostels, town halls, etc., along the route. It is the pilgrim's only proof that the journey has been made, and without it a 'Compostela' will not be issued in Santiago. At most hostels, accommodation will not be offered unless a pilgrim passport is being carried. They are available from the Confraternity of St James (if you are a member), the Cathedral at Le Puy, Roncesvalles monastery, and many other places along the route.

Transport

Reaching Le Puy with bicycles can be difficult, as can returning from Santiago. It is possible to take bicycles on the train in France, but we found it almost impossible to accompany them all the way and were not prepared to be separated from them. It is possible to fly with your bike, but we have heard so many horror stories of bikes being severely damaged in transit that we dismissed this possibility. In Spain it is now possible to send your bike ahead by road and travel by train, but the logistics of this, especially the transport of baggage, made it out of the question. We finally decided to use the excellent services of the European Bike Express, a coach firm that will take you and your bike (which is carried in a large trailer behind the coach) across France. We travelled to Valence in the Rhone valley (ask the European Bike Express for a list of their drop-off points), and then used a local coach firm (C Rhodaniens) to take our bikes and us from the Gare Routière in Valence to St Agrève, about 80km from Le Puy, and rode the rest. On completion of the pilgrimage we travelled on an ALSA National Bus Company coach with our bikes from Santiago to Bilbao (we could also have gone to Irun). It is necessary to book in advance with ALSA as only two bikes per journey can be accommodated. We then cycled north round the Spanish and French coast to Bayonne where the European Bike Express met us and brought us back to England. The transport throughout was quick and comfortable, and without exception the drivers were helpful and stored our bikes with the utmost care and no resulting damage. The only request was for us to turn our handlebars through 90 degrees, so have an Allen key handy.

When to Go
There is no perfect time to make the pilgrimage to Santiago. Everyone will give you a long list of pros and cons for every time of the year, but many people, like us, are constrained by outside influences. Travel in winter is virtually impossible. The mountain passes are closed more often than not. In springtime (until May) the weather will be a little warmer, but you can expect snow in the mountains and much of the accommodation may be closed. On our May 2004 pilgrimage we encountered lying snow, hailstorms, torrential

rain, gale-force winds, fog and a few days of warm sunshine. In summer expect temperatures of 40ºC across the Meseta in Spain, with refuges and hotels full of Spanish walkers using a short portion of the route for a ready-made walking holiday. Autumn sees temperatures falling and refuges and hotels less full, but expect to encounter severe weather at times in the mountains. If I were able to choose the perfect time to make the pilgrimage, I think I would choose a period between mid-May and mid-July, and expect some extremely cold nights but pleasant daytime temperatures for cycling.

It is essential to give yourself enough time to make the journey without undue hurry. As it is unlikely that you will do it twice, you should leave sufficient time each day to visit places of interest along the way and still finish your day's ride with some energy left for sightseeing. Walkers tend to leave their overnight halt at first light, but cyclists need not do this, as even in the blistering heat of the Meseta they create some breeze themselves and can complete a 50km stage comfortably by early afternoon when the sun is at its zenith. We found that the ideal time to find accommodation in Spain was at about 2pm, when streets were quiet at the beginning of the siesta and many pilgrims were still on the road. If you leave it until late afternoon, you may find yourself being turned away, especially in high season.

Food and Drink

We made it our policy never to carry more than one day's food with us, in the form of an emergency meal (dried food). Each day we were able to purchase some form of food – either salad items or a cheap restaurant meal. We had no difficulty in France, where even on Sundays many food shops were open in the morning, but in Spain it was often difficult to purchase raw materials and much simpler to eat in a café or restaurant at a very similar price. Remember, too, that in some areas of Spain water is turned off between 8am and 8pm. We always carried two water bottles each, and a carton of fruit juice which was readily available everywhere. Bars where you can refill your drinking bottles are found in almost every village along the route in France, but much less frequently in Spain, except in the towns.

In Spain, eating hours are also very different. Many bars and cafés do not open until 10.30am and serve lunch from 2pm. Evening meals are often available until 8.30pm or 9pm at the earliest, and we found a couple of places where food was not served until 11pm.

Noise

Finally, a word of warning. France is a land where everyone seems to retire to bed at about 10pm and even the church clocks are silenced at night. But everything changes the moment you reach Spain, where the noise you experience may be startling. The different eating hours mean that whole families take to the streets at midnight, after their evening meal, and stay up talking (and shouting) to each other for several hours. If you manage to stay in a refuge, expect the walkers to be up soon after 5am. So if you want to enjoy a few hours of peaceful, well-earned sleep each night, you are strongly advised to invest in a pair of sturdy earplugs (they will also protect you from the snorers!).

Language

It is best to assume that no one you meet on the entire journey will speak any English. Of course this will not be true, but, inevitably, when you need help there will be no English-speaking people available. Try to learn a little French and Spanish before you embark on the pilgrimage. Apart from being useful in emergencies, it will also enhance your enjoyment of the journey enormously.

Local people will appreciate your attempts to speak their language and can be very patient while you stumble through whatever you want to say. Whatever you do, do not shout at them in English. It does nothing for Anglo–French–Spanish relations and sours the ground for future pilgrims. There is a short glossary of terms in Appendix 4.

Money

Life in mainland Europe is much easier since the introduction of the euro.

21

There is no problem changing money at borders and it is very easy to compare prices everywhere. Unfortunately, the English must still put up with the task of money changing. The easiest way to do this is by using one of the thousands of ATM machines to be found along the route. Check that the logo on your card matches those displayed on the machine, choose the language you want to deal in and follow the instructions. If you have sufficient funds and do not ask for too much at one time, the machine will spout out your money. If you have any trouble, remove your card and go immediately into the bank or post office that houses the machine and explain your problem. Do not persist in pushing your card into the machine, because after three unsuccessful attempts the ATM will retain it.

Topography

Essentially this is a mountainous journey. There are a few riverside sections with gentle gradients, but do not expect this ride to be easy.

The first few stages climb in excess of 1300m and cross the Massif Central, a high, windswept volcanic plateau incised by deep gorges. It is an unforgiving place with little shelter and few centres of habitation. The journey along the Lot valley, in contrast, is easy, enjoyable riding through lush landscape. Here one rides between high limestone cliffs that tower above the river where whitewater rafting is a favourite sport. Once the Lot river is left behind, the rolling countryside of the Gers is encountered. Although this region is not as wild or dramatic as the Massif Central, it is equally demanding of

Estaing – in the Lot gorge (Stage 4)

the cyclist, with numerous short steep hills rolling on into the distance. When the foothills of the Pyrenees are reached, the climbing becomes more serious, with altitudes exceeding 1200m. Weather can again be a problem, with frequent storms and high winds.

Once in Spain, Navarre is, by contrast, a region of rolling countryside predominantly covered in scrub which eventually gives way to the vineyards of the Rioja. Here the slopes are less steep, apart from the ascent of the Montes de Oca. Soon afterwards, having passed through Burgos, the high plateau of the Meseta is encountered. This is a land of extremes, where the treeless terrain provides no shelter for the cyclist from high winds in winter and blistering heat and electric storms in summer. Towns and villages are well scattered and often appear derelict.

Once through the Meseta the route crosses the Montes de León, which contain the highest point of the whole pilgrimage, well over 1300m. This is harsh countryside where an eye needs to be kept on the weather at all times. After Ponferrada the final high mountain range, the Cantabrians, must be crossed, again reaching over 1300m. From here to Santiago de Compostela the gradients ease, but even on the final day the route crosses a long series of ridges and valleys before it reaches its final destination.

USING THIS GUIDE

This guide splits the route into 27 daily stages, but these are purely arbitrary. Information on places to stay along the stages, as well as at the end of each, are included so that cyclists may split the route according to their own needs and still have somewhere to stay.

The distance to be cycled each day is given in brackets at the beginning of each stage and is accurate to within 5km, depending on the number of 'off-the-track' places visited each day. After each place name in bold type, the elevation in metres is given, followed by brackets in which the first figure describes the distance travelled, and the second figure describes the distance to Santiago de Compostela. When tracing the route shown on the maps in the book, place names in **bold** type in the text give the route for the day 'at a glance'. Text in ordinary type gives directions and road conditions, text in *italics* gives information about facilities along the way, and text in brown type describes places and things of interest that can be visited on the route.

Road numbers were correct at the time of going to press, but both the French and Spanish authorities have a habit of changing them at will. Directions are usually given to left or right, but where there is difficulty a compass direction is also included.

The maps provided to accompany each day's ride are purely schematic, but roughly to the same scale. They

Molinaseca – medieval pilgrim bridge (Stage 22/23)

should provide enough visual information to give 'at a glance' guidance at awkward junctions, etc. It cannot be stressed too strongly that a set of IGN maps to cover the French section of the route and Michelin maps, for want of anything better, to cover the Spanish route are essential.

The Spanish authorities have recently introduced a new method of turning left off a main road. A slip-road is built to the right which turns at right angles to the main road and crosses it or passes under or over it. These slip-roads are usually well signed. In this guide they are usually described as 'slip right to turn left' and will quickly become evident.

The altitude profiles which accompany each stage should give the cyclist an idea of the terrain to be crossed, but many small yet stiff climbs simply could not be included for fear of making the cross-section look like a saw blade!

STAGE 1

Le Puy to Saugues (46km)

Route	A baptism of fire with an extremely steep climb out of Le Puy and a very long ascent from Monistrol. Hills all the way.
Surfaces	Good throughout, although the descent through St Privat d'Allier needs some care after rain.
See	The whole of Le Puy and the ancient quarter of Saugues with its Tour des Anglais and Church of St Medard.
Warning	The roads around Le Puy can be very busy (take care). Stop and allow rims to cool on the steep descent into the Allier gorge.

Le Puy 625m (0/1552)

There are gîtes d'étape, restaurants, bars, banks, shops, bike shops, supermarkets and a campsite. There are also many hotels, but the greatest welcome will be from the sisters at the Maison St François, Rue St Mayol below Notre Dame de France (04 71 04 07 36) – book in advance. A second gîte d'étape is at 29 Rue des Capucins (04 71 04 28 74). Pilgrims can stay at the Grand Séminaire, 4 Rue Saint-George (04 71 09 93 10). There is also a branch of the Amis St Jacques just below the cathedral. Open

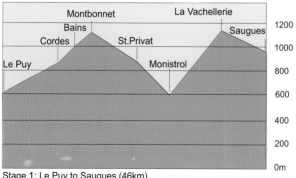

Stage 1: Le Puy to Saugues (46km)

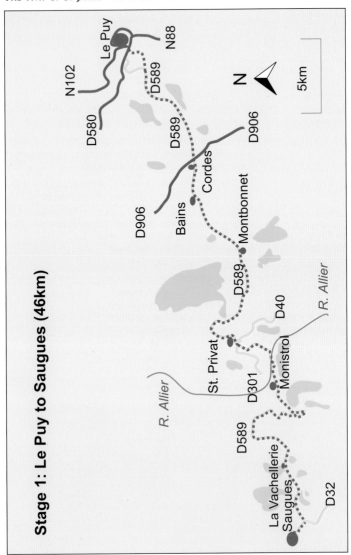

Stage 1: Le Puy to Saugues (46km)

*most evenings for sustenance and support before your
journey, it is a good place to meet fellow pilgrims whom
you will probably encounter again along the way. Have
your pilgrim passport stamped (with a 'tampon') in the
cathedral sacristy.*

This is a town to spend some time in. Visit the cathedral
to see the black virgin and the cloisters, and climb up
to the pinnacle church of St Michel d'Aiguilhe built on
an extinct volcanic plug. For a breathtaking view of the
city, climb inside the Notre Dame de France statue, made
from cannons melted down after the battle of Sebastopol,
and on foot explore the old town with its network of
twisting cobbled streets, ancient pilgrim hospitals and
weirdly carved keystones.

Leave Le Puy from the Place du Plot. Ride west up the
Rue St Jacques, cross the Boulevard St Louis, which can
be busy, and climb the Rue des Capucins. Turn right,
then left into the Rue de Compostelle, which becomes
the Rue des Pèlerins as it climbs very steeply above the
town, with excellent views of Le Puy and its volcanic
landscape. A factory is soon passed on the right as the
road becomes less steep. Keep to the tarmac (do not turn
left onto the GR65) until it meets the wider D589, which
undulates and climbs until it reaches a crossroads with
the D906. Go straight over into

Cordes 889m (10/1542)
No facilities.

This wide, quiet, well-surfaced road will be followed all
the way to Saugues. Ride straight on, still climbing, for
another 3km into

Bains 1006m (13/1539)
*Hotel Archer (04 71 57 52 38), chambre d'hôte (04 71
57 51 79 and 06 83 59 93 47), bar, restaurant and shops.*
See the church, which has frescoes inside and animal
sculptures round the door. It is dedicated to Ste Foy of
Conques.

Montbonnet – the climb before St Privat

This is the entrance to the Gévaudan, a wild moorland area famous for the legend of its man-eating beast, which might in fact have been France's first serial killer. The road continues to climb to

Montbonnet 1108m (16/1536)
Gîtes d'étape (04 71 57 50 82 or 04 71 57 51 03), camping, small bar and telephone. There is a bus shelter on the left-hand side of the road that would suffice as a refreshment stop in bad weather.

The road now begins to level out followed by a steep descent in wide sweeps to the town of

St Privat d'Allier 890m (24/1528)
Here can be found the Hotel de la Vieille Auberge (04 71 57 20 56), shops, restaurants and a campsite. There is also a gîte d'étape in the old École Chrétien (04 71 57 25 50).
The road through the village is narrow and winding with an indifferent surface. It is worth dismounting to explore the narrow alleyways, some with stupendous views of the Allier gorge.

The next 6km is an extremely steep but exhilarating descent on a narrow and, at times, busy road. The surface is subject to severe weather conditions in winter, and if badly patched may be unpleasant to cycle on. Care should be taken as the road dips into

Monistrol d'Allier 619m (30/1522)

Gîte d'étape communal (04 71 57 24 14), gite d'étape La Tsabone (04 71 06 17 23 or 06 03 02 19 01), gite d'étape Au Ricochet (04 71 57 20 97) and also Hotel des Gorges (06 84 04 88) and Hotel Restaurant Le Pain de Sucre (04 71 57 24 50) and a campsite in the town, all of which welcome pilgrims. There are also shops and a restaurant.

This gem of a little town, dominated by a hydroelectric power plant, straddles the River Allier. There are opportunities for white-water rafting and canoeing on the river, as well as walking on a multitude of well-marked paths in the woodland that abounds. A new road has been built, bypassing the centre of the village and crossing the river by means of a fine new bridge.

Monistrol d'Allier – the climb towards Saugues

29

The church, on the old road through the village, has an interesting carving of a pilgrim on a cross, although it may be locked.

Leave Monistrol keeping to the D589 over the new river bridge. Do not take the walkers' track to the right, but keep to the new tarmac road which, for the first couple of kilometres, climbs gently in a southerly direction, with the river gurgling on your right. Having crossed the river at a right-hand hairpin, the road steepens considerably and climbs above the river in a northerly direction. After another 3km ignore the road to the right (to Escluzels). Soon the GR65 (red and white markers) strikes off to the left to Montaure and Roziers, but there is no need for cyclists to follow it, as this is the walkers' track, steep and rough in places, and will rejoin the D589 just after La Vachellerie. Now look for a very welcome picnic area further along on the left-hand side of the road. This marks the halfway point of the ascent. The whole of this climb is well sheltered by trees and there are plenty of opportunities to rest and admire the stunning views of the Allier gorge. Having reached

La Vachellerie 1150m (39/1513)
No facilities.

The climb continues without any signs of easing, but when the road turns west for a kilometre, the gradient reduces. However, the road is still undulating as it reaches the high plateau of the Gévaudan, where it is still common to see shepherds guarding their flocks of sheep and goats. The road continues in a westerly direction for another 5km until a wide valley appears below and to the right, in the centre of which stands your destination. Sweep steeply right, down into the valley, following clear direction signs for Saugues, which is reached in a couple of kilometres. On entering Saugues, the road becomes the town's main street.

Saugues 960m (46/1506)

There are two hotels, the Hotel de la Terrasse (04 71 77 83 10) and the Hotel des Tours Neuves (04 71 77 82 60), chambres d'hôtes and two gîtes d'étape. One of these is large with chalet-type accommodation, and is situated alongside the stadium beyond the campsite below the town (04 71 77 81 21) (it is due to be replaced by a new one during 2005). There is a smaller private gîte d'étape (04 71 77 83 45) on the left above the town. There is simple accommodation at the Centre d'Accueil (04 71 77 60 97) and the tourist office has a list of accommodation. Nevertheless, rooms are scarce here and it is advisable to book in advance. Restaurants, a post office, banks, ATM, shops and a supermarket can all be found.

This is an attractive country market town with stone buildings and a large lake. The Church of St Medard is worth a visit, as is the Tour des Anglais, although the latter may be closed. The 12th-century pilgrim hospital, with statue of St Jacques, is now an old people's home.

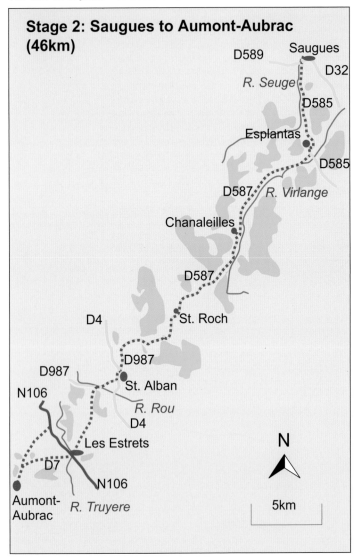

Stage 2: Saugues to Aumont-Aubrac (46km)

STAGE 2
Saugues to Aumont-Aubrac (46km)

Route	Very isolated and quiet for most of the stage. The way is undulating with a number of exposed, long climbs.
Surfaces	Good, although tarmac may be fragmenting on exposed stretches.
See	The romantic ancient chapel of St Roch and the Romanesque church at St Alban-sur-Limagnole.

Leave **Saugues** in a southerly direction by the D585 signed to St Alban with the river on your right. This is a straight, easy road which climbs gently until you spy the tower of a château directly ahead. Here the road swings left, then sharp right via a short steep hill to enter the village of

Esplantas 1075m (52/1500)
Bar, but little else to detain the pilgrim.

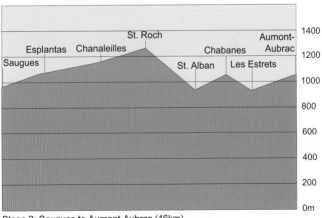

Stage 2: Saugues to Aumont-Aubrac (46km)

Esplantas

Immediately after the village take the right fork at the T-junction onto the D587 – this hilly road through moorland and valley is studded with wild flowers. After 8km take a right turn into the village of

Chanaleilles 1150m (61/1491)
Here there is a welcoming bar, shop and a gîte d'étape (04 71 74 41 63).

Continue in a southwesterly direction on the D587 out of Chanaleilles, climbing steeply through woodland interspersed with mountain pasture. During spring and summer these meadows are carpeted with wild flowers. After 4km there is a track to the left signed to Le Sauvage (gîte d'étape, 04 71 74 40 30). Ignore this, unless you are desperate for a rest so early in the day, and continue along the D587. In a couple of kilometres the track from Le Sauvage will rejoin the road, and soon after, following a long hard climb, a chapel standing to the right of the road will be reached. This is dedicated to the patron saint of pilgrims

St Roch 1280m (69/1483)

Picnic benches outside the church and a good shelter alongside if the weather is inclement. There is also a drinking fountain.

One can imagine the grey stone church, which is often locked, being a most welcome sight for weary pilgrims in the Middle Ages, when it provided them with the only shelter and succour available. It was first built in 1198 and rededicated between 1562 and 1598. A new chapel was built early in the 19th century, but destroyed by a cyclone in 1897. In 1901 the existing chapel was erected.

The road numbering now changes and the road you are on becomes the D987, climbing one last ridge before gently descending into

St Alban-sur-Limagnole 950m (77/1475)

The town has hotels – the Hotel du Breuil (04 66 31 51 76) and the Relais Saint-Roc (04 66 31 55 48) – plus a gîte d'étape on the floor above the Hotel du Centre (04 66 31 50 04), if it is operating. There is also a campsite

St Alban-
sur-Limagnole –
12th-century church

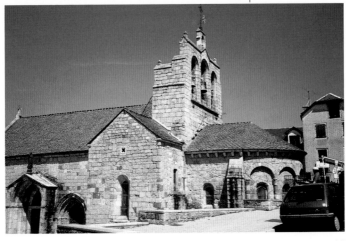

open from March to November at the far side of the town. There are numerous shops, bars and restaurants. The beautiful 12th-century Romanesque church in polychrome stone is worth a visit, if only to see the exquisitely carved capitals.

Leave the town in a westerly direction by the D987 for 2km until it crosses the river on a new bridge. Here turn left at an awkward junction onto a narrow minor road which climbs steeply to the hamlet of

Chabanes-Planes 1041m (82/1470)
No facilities.

The road now levels out before plunging down to

Les Estrets 940m (86/1466)
A gîte d'étape (04 66 45 61 90), chambre d'hôte, telephone and drinking fountain can be found here.
The Knights of St John of Jerusalem once administered this very ancient settlement. There are some interesting carvings in the 19th-century church.
Cross the N106, turn right and ride parallel to it for 200m, then cross the **Pont des Estrets**. If the road is open, climb west across the high plateau to Aumont Aubrac. If not, turn right to join the N108, turn left onto it and in a couple of kilometres take a left turn to **Le Vestit**. Ride straight through the hamlet before rejoining the road into

Aumont-Aubrac 1050m (92/1460)
This small market town, which has its origins in Roman times, has four hotels, restaurants and excellent small food shops as well as two gîtes d'étape. A new gîte has been opened alongside a hotel (04 66 42 99 00) – the other (04 66 42 90 25) tends to be very busy, so phone in advance. The Hôtel Prunière (04 66 42 85 52) welcomes pilgrims and has secure cycle storage. There is a railway station here and a tourist office in the town hall. The post office has an ATM and there is also a bank here.

Ride down to the lower end of the village to visit the recently restored church dedicated to St Etienne and admire its stained glass.

Aumont-Aubrac – wild narcissus on the Marferide

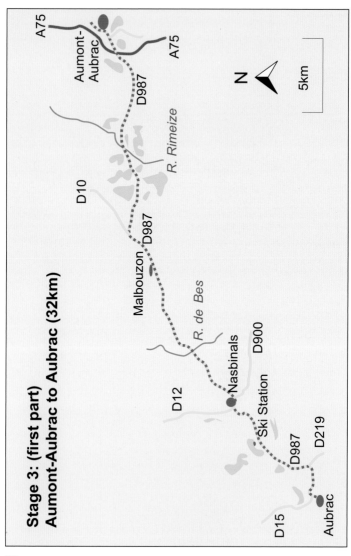

Stage 3: (first part)
Aumont-Aubrac to Aubrac (32km)

STAGE 3
Aumont-Aubrac to Estaing (76km)

Route	The first half of this stage continues the climb across the Massif Central on roads which are exposed during bad weather, which is frequent. Once the descent from Aubrac is undertaken, the lush vegetation of the Lot valley is encountered and cycling becomes much easier.
Surfaces	The roads around Aubrac are subject to frost damage, and the back roads between St Côme d'Olt and Estaing are of poor quality, though perfectly rideable.
See	The pilgrim church at Nasbinals, the twisted spire in St Côme d'Olt, the amazing decoration at the Église de Perse near Espalion, and the church within the tower of St Pierre, Bessuéjouls. The day is one long sightseeing adventure.
Warning	The descent from Aubrac is exhilarating, but remember to allow brakes to cool at regular intervals. The centre of Espalion can be very busy with heavy lorries.

Leave **Aumont-Aubrac** in a westerly direction on the D987, which is followed for most of the day. It is a

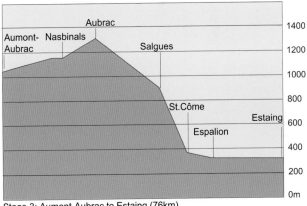

Stage 3: Aumont-Aubrac to Estaing (76km)

good, wide, well-surfaced road with little traffic. After 2km cross the A75 AutoRoute and climb steadily through woodland for about 6km. Without warning the woodland comes to an abrupt end and you find yourself on the wide open spaces of the Margeride, a strange plateau, reminiscent of Dartmoor, which looks as though someone has dumped enormous piles of rock all over it, although they are natural phenomena. In springtime the fields here are carpeted with wild daffodils.

Malbouzon 1175m (106/1446)

Bar and restaurant.
With its wide streets, Malbouzon is the first town of any size to be reached. The next 9km across the Margeride are very exposed, with no signs of habitation, but a sharp descent and climb leads into

Nasbinals 1180m (115/1437)

This is a busy market town with four hotels – La Randonée (04 66 32 54 07), Le Bastide (04 66 32 56 82), La Route d'Argent (04 66 32 50 03) and the Hotel de France (04 66 32 50 19) – and three gîtes d'étape (04 66 32 59 47 – municipal, 04 66 32 15 60 – private, 04 66 32 50 42 – Centre d'Accueil) in the vicinity. There is also a municipal campsite. It is easy to find restaurants, shops, a bank, pharmacy and a market.

A stamp for your pilgrim passport can be obtained from the priest who lives next door to the 11th-century Romanesque church, which has a modern statue of St Jacques and one or two remarkable carvings. The mairie will also provide a pilgrim stamp. If food is needed, this is the last opportunity to buy any for 35km.

Now begins a long climb to the hilltop village of Aubrac. Once again the route is very exposed in places, with little shelter in inclement weather. After a hard climb the Station de Ski is reached in 4km. There is a bar/restaurant here but little else. 5km further along the route is Aubrac col (1340m), where the road swings left into the centre of

Aubrac 1307m (124/1428)

One of the highest villages on the French section of the pilgrimage route, this very small community has two expensive hotels, the Royal Aubrac (05 65 44 28 41) and the Hotel de la Domerie (05 65 44 28 42), and restaurants but no shops. There is a tiny tourist office and a gîte d'étape in the medieval Tour des Anglais (05 65 44 21 15), but it does not open until 5.00pm. A pilgrim shelter can be found on the square – a necessity in this high, exposed place.

Do not leave without visiting the 13th-century church dedicated to Notre-Dame des Pauvres, with its walls of stupendous thickness, all that is left of the 12th-century monastery.

A long, mainly downhill ride of 26km now follows. It is possible to branch off left after a kilometre to visit the pretty village of St Chély d'Aubrac (808m) (hotels, restaurants, shop, post office, camping and gîte d'étape on the walker's route), but this entails a very steep descent followed by the inevitable ascent out of the village, which is picturesque but not breathtaking. (If this detour is taken, be sure to cross the bridge in the village – failure to do so can result in a very stiff climb to regain the D987.)

If you do not want to visit St Chély, stay on the D987 and descend with breathtaking views across the Lot valley to the mountains of the Causse Mejean and the Cevennes National Park. Having reached

Salgues 917m (142/1410)

bar, restaurant and 16th-century church.

The route begins its 8km descent into St Côme d'Olt. The road steepens considerably on this stretch and it is wise to stop at least once to allow the rims to cool.

St Côme d'Olt 385m (150/1402)

Gîte d'étape del Roumiou housed in a medieval tower (06 35 59 16 05) where your bicycle can be stored in the basement next to the showers – key at hardware shop. An

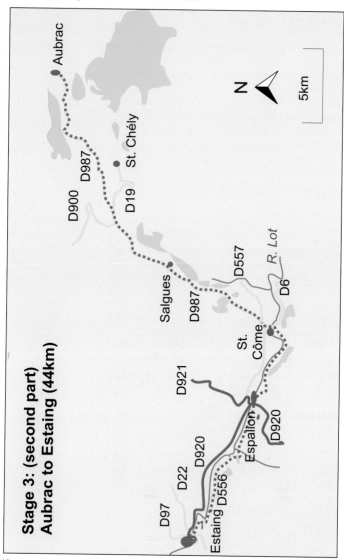

**Stage 3: (second part)
Aubrac to Estaing (44km)**

excellent new private gîte d'étape/chambre d'hôte (05 65 48 28 06) has now opened in the town centre and will provide evening meals. Accommodation is also available at the Hotel des Voyageurs (05 65 44 27 05) and the Hotel de la Vallée (05 65 44 27 40). Shops, restaurants, tourist office, campsite, post office and a bank can be found. The town hall is the place to have your pilgrim passport stamped. Be prepared for everywhere except the gîte to be shut on Sundays.

This exquisite, partially walled medieval town has a 15th-century church with an alarmingly twisted spire. Situated on the banks of the River Lot, its cobbled lanes and half-timbered houses are a joy and may tempt you to linger.

Leave St Côme d'Olt by crossing the River Lot (look for pilgrim carving on the bridge) and turn immediately right

*St Côme d'Olt –
the twisted spire*

43

onto a country lane that follows the Lot valley through pleasant leafy suburbs for 5km to the outskirts of Espalion. On a bank to the left of the lane can be seen the **Église de Perse**. Turn left onto a rough track to reach the church. This exquisitely decorated 11th-century church dedicated to St Hilarion deserves lengthy exploration. Return to the lane and ride the few hundred metres into the centre of

Espalion 342m (156/1396)

There are two hotels, the Moderne (05 65 44 05 11) and the Hotel de France (05 65 44 06 13), the gîte d'étape communal (05 65 51 10 30) and the Halte St. Jacques (05 65 66 35 61), a campsite, cycle repair shop, other shops, restaurants, banks and a post office.

This is a very busy town where several important roads meet and cross the River Lot, as they have since Roman times. The parish church has an imposing façade but the interior is drab. The museum opposite has travelling exhibitions, and the staff at the town hall are most helpful to pilgrims and will stamp your pilgrim passport. The pilgrim bridge is very photogenic.

Keep to the south side of the River Lot and take the road immediately to the right of the Hotel de Ville (D556). Care is needed here, as it is easy to miss this road. After 3km take a lane to the left, signed Bessuéjouls. Within 400m take a rough track to the left (there is no need to go into Bessuéjouls village) which in 200m leads to the

Church of St Pierre, Bessuéjouls 335m (160/1392)

Gîte d'étape (05 65 48 20 71).

This is one of the most beautiful churches on the whole pilgrimage. The real gem of the building is a tiny chapel on the first floor of the tower. Here there are 9th-century tableaux and capitals with wonderful carvings. It is the hours well spent here and in Estaing that make the day such a busy and time-consuming one.

Retrace your steps to the D556 and turn left for Estaing. The road, which is a mixture of flat riding and short hills, crosses farmland devoted to market gardening rather than the cattle ranching of the Margeride. The scenery is fine, with the river away to your right, and in 6km, on reaching

Verrières 450m (166/1386)
Bar.

the road turns sharp right at a T-junction and runs high along the left bank of the beginning of the Lot gorge. After 2km turn right at the junction with the D22 and cross the ancient bridge over the Lot to enter

Estaing 320m (168/1384)
There are two hotels, Aux Armes d'Estaing (05 65 44 70 20) and Saint-Fleuret (05 65 44 01 44), a gîte d'étape communal (05 65 44 03 22), campsite close by, restaurants, banks and plenty of shops and a supermarket, but if you stay at the Hospitalité Saint Jacques (05 65 44 19 00) none of this need worry you. You will be cared for and fed in peace and tranquillity, and sent out refreshed in spirit and body the following day. Even your bicycle will be stored safely in their garage. The distinctive red stamp of the Hospitalité will be put into your pilgrim passport when you sign the visitors' book (the 'Livre d'Or').

Estaing is another beautiful small medieval town with a mighty 16th-century château towering over it. The château is now a convent but can still be visited. The 15th-century church of St Fleuret has an interesting pilgrim carving. Narrow streets twist and turn below it, and the promenade makes a relaxing place to sit beside the River Lot. This is a day to savour, not to rush through.

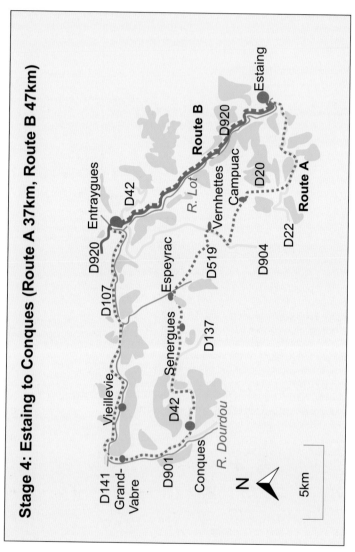

Stage 4: Estaing to Conques (Route A 37km, Route B 47km)

STAGE 4

Estaing to Conques
(Route A 37km, Route B 47km)

Route	There are two possible routes on this stage. Route A is very hilly with difficult map reading, but includes a fascinating church at Campuac. Route B is flat, along the Lot gorge, and easy to follow.
Surfaces	Route A can be difficult beyond Campuac if the map is not strictly followed. Route B is on excellent roads which can be busy as far as Entraygues.
See	The artwork inside the church at Campuac, and the cathedral, treasury and whole village of Conques.
Warning	Map reading becomes difficult immediately beyond Campuac, as roads on the ground do not seem to tally with those on the map.

ROUTE A

Leave **Estaing** by the medieval bridge over the Lot, and at the first junction take the D22, right, for Campuac. For the next 8km the road climbs, often steeply, with many hairpin bends, before levelling out as it nears

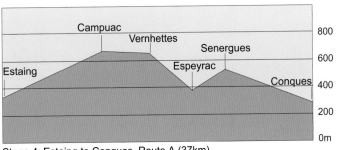

Stage 4: Estaing to Conques, Route A (37km)

Campuac 675m (180/1372)

Restaurant and bar.

The church here is worth visiting. The exterior is simple, but the interior is filled with beautiful modern stained glass and many modern sculptures and ecclesiastical pieces.

Note The route between Campuac and Espeyrac is very complex, as there are many minor roads with little to distinguish them and the IGN map is difficult to follow. It is often very hard to tell which roads are on the map and which are not. If you are at all unsure it may be safer to take the D20, to the right just before entering Campuac, follow this as far as Golinhac, and then turn left onto the D519 to Espeyrac.

Leave the town by a small lane, signed GR65, at the far right corner of the square. Turn right at the first main road, the D904 (not signed), and ignore any other signs which may be there. In 2km enter the hamlet of

Vernhettes 661m (186/1366)

No facilities.

Turn left for **Campagnac** on the D519. This road descends more and more steeply until it reaches the D42 on the outskirts of

Espeyrac 369m (191/1361)

Hotel/Restaurant de la Vallée (05 65 69 87 61) as well as a gîte d'étape (05 65 72 93 46 or 05 65 69 87 46), bar and shop.

If the church is open look for the statues of St Roch, and St Peter with a cockerel.

If you want to visit this small town for refreshments, turn right and climb for a kilometre. If not, turn left onto the D42 and begin an 8km climb through the ancient village of

Senergues 506m (195/1357)

Hotel, restaurant, bars, shops, post office and a private gîte d'étape (05 65 72 91 56).

Inside the Church of St Martin is yet another St Roch statue, and the church itself is built on the site of a 9th-century priory.

You meet the D137 2km after leaving this village. Go straight along it and within another 2km (the road has now become the D42) begin a 6km descent into

Conques 280m (205/1347)

Ignore the 'No Entry' sign (for cars) and drop directly down the main cobbled street to the cathedral.

ROUTE B

Leave Estaing in a northerly direction on the D920. The road climbs gently as it enters the Lot gorge, with the river on the left, then begins a gradual descent. There are a number of places that tempt the cyclist to stop to admire the view, but beware of traffic, as this can be a busy road with motorists also admiring the view! No villages or towns of any size are encountered until

Entraygues sur Truyère 222m (185/1367)

All facilities, including the Hotel de la Truyère (05 65 44 51 10), Hotel de Deux Vallées (05 65 44 52 15), Hotel du Centre (05 65 44 51 19) and the Lion d'Or (05 65 44 50 01). There are also two campsites.

Stage 4: Estaing to Conques, Route B (47km)

This is a busy little market town with a château built on an island at the confluence of the rivers Lot and Truyère. It is a favourite destination for French holidaymakers, as the scenery hereabouts is truly spectacular. Entraygues is the last town of any size from which provisions can be bought for the rest of the day.

Ride through the town on the D920 until you reach the first bridge over which traffic is permitted to cross the Truyère. Cross this and immediately take a sharp left turn onto the D107 (not the D920), riding back on the opposite bank of the river. Follow this road for many kilometres as it hugs the bank of the river to your left. After about 10km the road number changes to the D141. Continue to follow it until a lunch stop is found at

Vieillevie 210m (200/1352)
Bar and restaurant.

Leave this medieval village, keeping on the D141 until, after approximately 7km, a modern bridge can be seen spanning the River Lot. Cross this bridge, which is

Entraygues – at the confluence of rivers

clearly signed to Grand-Vabre and Conques, taking the D901. The river flowing immediately on your right is the Dourdou, a pretty tributary of the Lot, often lined with campsites promoting canoeing and white-water rafting. The flower-bedecked village of

Vieillevie – author and blossom

Grand-Vabre 275m (209/1342)
bars and restaurants,

need not detain you, as in another 6km you will have arrived in the medieval gem of the region,

Conques 280m (215/1337)
Accommodation, including an evening meal, is available at the SCOP Saint Norbert, Accueil de l'Abbaye Ste Foy (05 65 69 89 43) or, surprisingly cheaply, at the Auberge St Jacques (05 65 72 82 47) opposite the entrance to the cathedral (bicycles stored in the bar at night). There is also a gîte d'étape (05 65 72 82 98) and nearby campsite. Restaurants, bars and shops abound (post office but no bank).

Conques – Abbey tympanum

Conques is rated one of the most beautiful sites in France. It is certainly a lovely medieval village, but it can be overrun with tourists. The best time to see it is in the late evening, when the setting sun brings out the colours of the cathedral's tympanum, depicting the harrowing of hell, or in the early morning, when the cobbled streets are still empty and echoing and wisps of mist drift down the valley – then Conques is as it must have been during the Middle Ages. A visit to the cathedral is a 'must', if only to see the alabaster 'glass' in the windows. The golden statue of Ste Foy in the treasury museum is the star attraction, if a little over the top. The story of how it arrived in Conques, though, is a fascinating one and gives an insight into medieval religious intrigue.

STAGE 5

Conques to Marcilhac-sur-Célé
(Route A 78km, Route B 75km)

Route	There are two possible routes on this stage. Route A is a long, hard section which begins with the steepest climb encountered so far. There is a second long steep climb up the 5km before Montredon, but the day does end with a long, spectacular flat ride along the Célé valley. The first long climb can be avoided by following Route B.
Surfaces	As far as Port d'Agrès on Route A, surfaces can be rough with plenty of potholes, but after this the road surfaces are good.
See	Go inside the St Roch chapel near Noailhac to see the stained glass (Route A). Figeac has a number of fine sites, including the monuments to Champollian and the Church of St Sauveur. The ruined priory at Espagnac and the remains of the abbey at Marcilhac-sur-Célé should certainly be visited.
Warning	The descent into Figeac and the journey through the town can be exceedingly busy. In places it may be better to dismount and push rather than compete with all the heavy trucks.

ROUTE A

Conques is a long straggling village descended by a winding cobbled street, the Rue Charlemagne, to the River Dourdou. Cross it using the medieval bridge next to the Auberge du Pont Romain (06 65 69 84 07) and climb the road which begins at the far side.

The next 6km is an unrelenting steep climb. There are some excellent views looking back to Conques, and considerable shade from overhanging trees if the weather is hot, but you will be heartily sick of the hill by the time you reach its summit close to the junction with the D606. Turn left here, but there is no need to go into

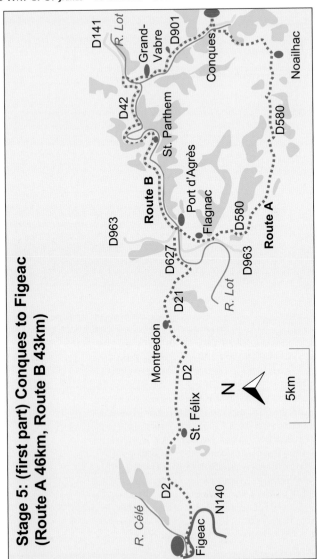

Stage 5: (first part) Conques to Figeac (Route A 46km, Route B 43km)

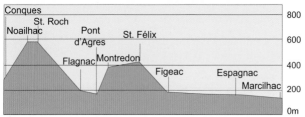

Stage 5: Conques to Marcilhac (78km)

Noailhac 595m (221/1331)
gîte d'étape (05 65 72 91 25) – key from café, restaurant,

unless you have some special reason. Instead, keep on the D580 to the right which quickly takes you to the chapel of

St Roch 595m (223/1329)
This beautiful isolated chapel, with an evocative statue of St Roch, the patron saint of pilgrims, on its façade also has a most attractive stained glass window inside and a picnic area opposite.

The road now climbs and plunges across hilly terrain with radio masts on the summits. After 8km, at **La Bessenoits**, ignore the road to the left into Decazeville (all facilities including cycle shop) but keep to the D580, signed Agnac. Decazeville, with its scars from open-cast mining, can clearly be seen below and to your left, but stay above it, on a badly surfaced road, through the suburb of **Agnac**.

The road now sweeps down for 4km in a series of hairpin bends until it reaches a junction with the D963. Turn right onto this road with the River Lot close by on your left. In 3km a diversion to the right and uphill takes you into the small sleepy town of

Flagnac 200m (236/1316)
There is no necessity to visit Flagnac unless supplies or refreshments are needed, but this is the first place offering

food and a bar since leaving Conques. Be aware that everything, including the bar, shuts at lunchtime.

Continue through the town. The road swings left and drops to rejoin the D963 just before

Port d'Agrès 185m (238/1314)
There is a hotel and bar immediately on the left over the bridge.

Cross the bridge and take the first road on the left (in 200m), the D627.

ROUTE B
If even the sight of Route A zigzagging its way out of Conques makes you shudder, a less strenuous variant is available. Cycle down and out of the village on the tarmac road, turning right onto the D901. Retrace the course of Stage 4's Route B for 6km as far as the bridge over the River Lot. Here, cross the bridge and turn left onto the D42.

This road follows the north bank of the River Lot, although it is by no means flat. After 8km the road bypasses St Parthem (shop) before winding its way through a series of tiny hamlets until the village of Port d'Agrès is reached at a T-junction with the D963. Turn right here and immediately left onto the D627, joining Route A.

The D627 keeps the River Lot on its left until it meets the D21 at Basse-Ville (no facilities). The climb out of the village, west along the D21, is long (5km) and steep but not as steep as the first kilometre suggests. After passing through

Montredon 396m (244/1308)
Gîte de Montredon (05 65 62 27 65), chambre d'hôte (05 65 34 38 20) bar and shop,

the road (now the D2) continues to undulate with some steady climbs and descents as far as

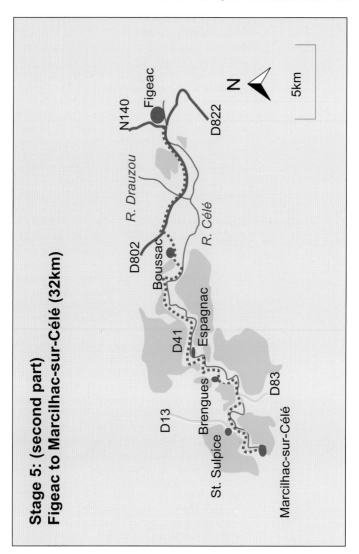

Stage 5: (second part)
Figeac to Marcilhac-sur-Célé (32km)

St Félix 422m (252/1300)
Restaurant (05 65 50 14 01).
The Church of St Radegonde, with its primitive 11th-century tympanum depicting the Garden of Eden, is worth a visit, although the interior may be locked. The church is just off the D2 but well signed and easily found.

Climb steeply out of the village until the D2 is rejoined. This now undulates with several lengthy climbs until it joins the N140 (turn right). This road can be very busy with heavy lorries as it descends to cross the River Célé at Figeac. Cross the river and turn right then immediately left to enter the old part of the town (beware the one-way system).

Figeac 194m (259/1293)
Figeac is a pleasant medieval town with many restored houses and all facilities, including eight hotels, a gîte d'étape (05 81 71 50 28) just outside town, a campsite, restaurants, banks, tourist office, shops, cycle shop and supermarkets, most of which close at lunchtime. It can be very busy. Although this was once an important pilgrim halt, present-day Figeac tends to shun pilgrims.
The Church of St Sauveur has a most interesting crypt with unusual decoration. Jean François Champollian, who deciphered the Rosetta stone, was born here and a small Cleopatra's needle and a floor bearing the Rosetta stone inscription are to be found in the old quarter.

Leave Figeac by the D802 in a westerly direction, keeping the River Célé on your left. (The immediate exit is confusing, as it turns away from the river, bearing right through suburban housing for 0.5km, but it is well signed to Cahors.) Pass supermarkets to the left and the Ratier factory to the right, and in 6km, at an awkward junction, turn left off the D802 onto the D41, again keeping the river immediately to your left. You are now entering the Célé gorge, which runs for 50km to join the Lot gorge, becoming ever more spectacular the further you enter it.
In 5km pass through the farming village of

Boussac 175m (269/1283)
No facilities.
There is an interesting pieta in the church dedicated to
St John the Baptist.

After 3km skirt the village of **Corn** (no facilities), dominated by its ruined château, for there is no need to stop
here, and another 7km further on, nestling on the far side
of a bridge over the Célé, you will see the remains of the
priory of

Espagnac 163m (279/1273)
*The possibility of overnight accommodation at a simple
three-roomed gîte d'étape (05 65 11 42 66) as well as a
bar and tearooms.*
It may be possible to visit the ancient ecclesiastical buildings of the 13th-century Priory of Val Paradis, which are
well worth a visit if you have time, as is the rest of this
tiny village.

*Figeac – Quercy-
style house*

59

But if you are not tired of the almost flat road, recross the bridge and turn left, continuing along the D41 through

Brengues 159m (283/1269)
Hotel de la Vallée (05 65 40 02 50), two chambres d'hôte (05 65 40 05 44 and 05 65 40 00 46), two campsites, kayak station with its tiny bar and shops.

Then enter

St Sulpice 154m (289/1263)
There is a chambre d'hôte (05 65 40 03 80) just outside the village as well as a campsite, shop and bar.
Here houses as well as the castle are built into the rock, and caves pockmark the valley sides.

Ride straight on until you reach the small town of

Marcilhac-sur-Célé 148m (293/1259)
There are two gîtes d'étape. One (05 65 40 61 43, bicycles stored inside) is built in the ruins of the Benedictine abbey which is itself well worth a visit. The other, Accueil

Marcilhac-sur-Célé – sharing a pilgrim meal

Gîtes d'étape *in the grounds of the abbey*

St. Pierre (06 34 36 54 60 or 05 81 24 06 30), has had new proprietors since 2014. There are campsites, chambres d'hôte, bars, a restaurant and shops.
Marcilhac-sur-Célé was once one of the wealthiest ecclesiastical communities in the region (it owned the magnificent town of Rocomadour), but it has seen better days and now has a rather mournful air. The Syndicate d'Initiative, also in the abbey grounds, is extremely helpful to pilgrims. The nearby caves of Bellevue are worth a visit, but there is a lengthy steep climb to reach them.

THE WAY OF ST JAMES – A CYCLISTS' GUIDE

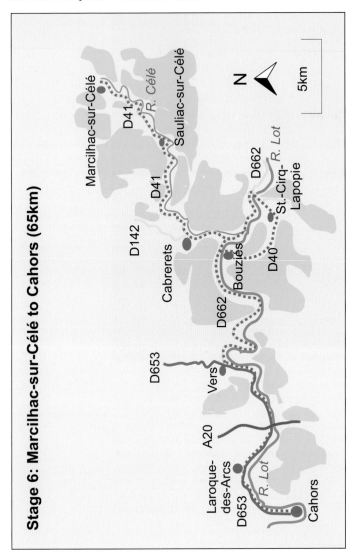

Stage 6: Marcilhac-sur-Célé to Cahors (65km)

STAGE 6
Marcilhac-sur-Célé to Cahors (65km)

Route	This is an easy day's riding with just one long ascent and descent in order to visit St-Cirq-Lapopie.
Surfaces	Generally good except for the descent from St-Cirq-Lapopie to Bouziès, which is narrow and can be frost damaged.
See	The strange 'Museum of the Unusual' (Musée d'insolité) at Sauliac-sur-Célé, the whole village of St-Cirq-Lapopie (although it may be seething with tourists) and the many fine sights in Cahors.
Warning	There are several short tunnels to ride through on this day's journey. Make sure your lights are working and that you keep right in to the edge of the road, as some of the tunnels are narrow with bends.

Leave **Marcilhac** in a westerly direction by the D41. The road now enters the most spectacular part of the Célé gorge, with high cliffs and a series of short road tunnels, through

Sauliac-sur-Célé 140m (300/1252)
No facilities.
Stop to look round the Musée d'insolité and search out the troglodyte chapel.
Ride beneath massive overhanging cliffs to reach

Cabrerets 130m (309/1243)
Two expensive hotels, the Hotel des Grottes (05 65 31 27 02) and the Auberge de la Sagne (05 65 31 26 62),

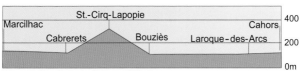

Stage 6: Marcilhac to Cahors (65km)

Sauliac-sur-Célé – Museum of the Unusual

gîte d'étape *Le Refuge du Célé (09 66 88 20 15)*, campsite, bars and shops.

Cabrerets has two châteaux, neither of which can be visited. If time permits, a visit to the Grotte de Pech-Merle and its museum is recommended. It is claimed that the cave paintings here are second only to Lascaux, but there is a lengthy steep climb to reach them, and the guided tour is long.

A further 4km brings you to the T-junction with the D662 where the Célé runs into the River Lot. Turn left onto the D662 and follow this busy road for 4km, keeping the River Lot to your right. At the sign for St-Cirq-Lapopie, turn right over the river bridge and climb very steeply into this famous village.

St-Cirq-Lapopie 304m (319/1233)
There are two expensive hotels, the Hotel de la Pélissaria (06 65 31 25 14) and L'Auberge du Sombral (05 65 31 26 08), a gîte d'étape (05 65 31 21 51), campsite, shops, restaurants and bars as well as a tourist office. There is also a gîte d'étape at Tour de Faure 2km away.

This is a tiny medieval village perched above the Lot gorge. It was once the home of woodturners, with many craftsmen plying their trade, and you may have to fight your way through throngs of tourists to see the place! The church is in a bad state of repair but renovation work is about to begin. The château ramparts provide fine views of the Lot valley.

Do not retrace your steps, but ride on along the D40 to Bouziès. This involves a short sharp climb to an awkward junction beside the coach park (bear right), followed by a fascinating ride along a terrace high on the side of the Lot gorge before descending spectacularly to

Bouziès 126m (329/1223)
Expensive hotel/restaurant, Les Falaises (05 65 31 26 83). Boat trips along the Lot and a tourist train are available here.

In the centre of the village turn right to cross the narrow suspension bridge over the Lot and turn left onto the D662, passing through the Defile of the English and beneath the English Château built into the rocks overhead. This busy and far less interesting road will lead you through

St Géry 122m (338/1214)
Expensive bar, restaurant and shops.

After crossing the rarely used railway line several times, the road leads into

Vers 119m (343/1209)
Hotel de la Truite Dorée (05 65 31 41 51), campsite, bar, restaurants and shops.
There has been a settlement here since the Bronze Age, and there are traces of the Roman aqueduct which served Cahors if you have time to look for them. A number of traffic-calming devices make the town difficult for cyclists and the roundabout (follow signs to Cahors – D653) is also awkward to negotiate.

*Laroque-des-Arcs –
perched chapel*

A small chapel will soon be seen perched on top of a pinnacle of rock ahead. This marks the entrance to the Gallo-Roman township of

Laroque-des-Arcs 115m (352/1200)

Restaurant, shops and bar.

There are some remains of the Roman aqueduct that transported water to Cahors here as well, but they are not signposted and awkward to find.

Soon after this the outskirts of Cahors appear, the city being reached in another 6km. Make the final section of this ride close to the river (do not climb steeply from the roundabout, but bear left where the road is obviously flatter). Ride as far as the second bridge from the left and turn right up the main street to the town centre.

Cahors 122m (358/1194)

All facilities. Cahors is a large, bustling commercial and market town with congested traffic, a convoluted one-way system and several hotels ranging in price. There are also several gîtes d'etapes and information about these may be obtained either at the pilgrim accueil on the Pont Philippe called the Octroi or from the accueil in the cathedral or the Tourist Office in the centre of the town who will provide an excellent town plan free of charge.

There are now two Pilgrim welcome points in Cahors between May and September. One is at the end of the Louis Philippe Bridge and the other is in the Cathedral. Between them they offer ideas for accommodation and food as well as spiritual support. Similar help should be available in 2006 at Figeac and Lascabanes. This is provided by the Amis de Saint Jacques de Quercy. The Cathedral of Saint Etienne has a magnificent 12th-century tympanum on the north side. The 183m-long Pont Valentré, whose towers are 40m high, claimed to be the finest fortified bridge in Europe, is worth close examination. The medieval quarter, once the financial heart of France, has a number of fine buildings and many more are being restored.

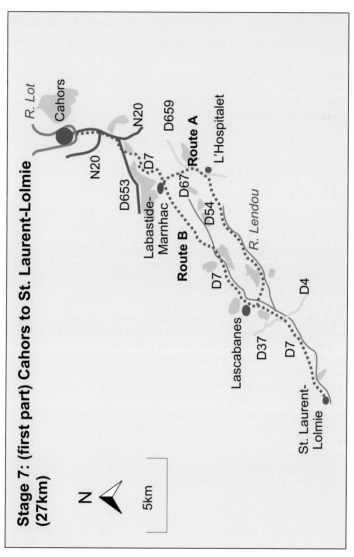

Stage 7: (first part) Cahors to St. Laurent-Lolmie (27km)

STAGE 7
Cahors to Moissac (61km)

Route	Easy riding with only one sizeable necessary hill all day. Two alternative routes, A and B, are given.
Surfaces	Very good.
See	The medieval town of Lauzerte and the beauty that is Moissac Abbey.
Warning	The N20 leaving Cahors is always busy. Take great care, especially negotiating the first roundabout.

Do not leave Cahors as most walking pilgrims do, by the Pont Valentré, but follow the main street through the town south to go over the Louis Phillipe bridge and leave on the N20, signed to Toulouse, passing numerous car showrooms and out-of-town supermarkets. **This short stretch of autoroute is very busy – take extreme care.** After 3km, at the second roundabout, turn right onto the D653, passing beneath a railway bridge. Within a kilometre take a left turn, the D7, which climbs steadily as far as

Labastide-Marnhac 257m (365/1187)
One gîte in the centre (05 65 21 03 13), as well as toilets, telephone and drinking fountain.

There are two alternative routes here, each as pleasant as the other.

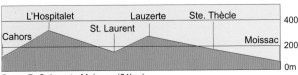

Stage 7: Cahors to Moissac (61km)

ROUTE A

In the village turn left immediately after the church onto the D67 to ride across open moorland before meeting the D659 at a T-junction in 3km. Turn right onto this road and in just over a kilometre reach the village of

L'Hospitalet 319m (369/1183)

Chambre d'hôte (05 65 21 02 83), campsite, restaurant and shop.
The 13th-century church choir was once a part of the pilgrim hospital. Collect your pilgrim stamp from the mairie.

Turn right here onto the D54. This is a beautiful valley road passing through farmland and gently descending for 10km until it reaches a minor crossroads with the D7.

ROUTE B

You do not need to enter the village of Labastide Marnhac, but simply stay on the D7 as it bypasses the community. If you have entered the village, do not turn left at the church, but ride straight ahead until the road meets the D7 just beyond the new mairie. Follow this as it descends gradually with long sweeping curves until it reaches the heavily restored but very pretty village of

Lascabanes 180m (376/1176)

Gîte d'étape (05 65 31 49 12 or 05 65 31 86 38), chambre d'hôte (05 65 31 82 51) and shops.
This Quercy village used to have a pilgrim hospital. See the 16th-century Church of St George and the 19th-century Chapel of St John.

Ride through the village, staying on the D7. Shortly the Route A road will join from the left. Keep straight ahead here for St Laurent-Lolmie and Lauzerte. This road, too, descends through a wide river valley devoted to melon growing, in 7km passing through the hamlet of

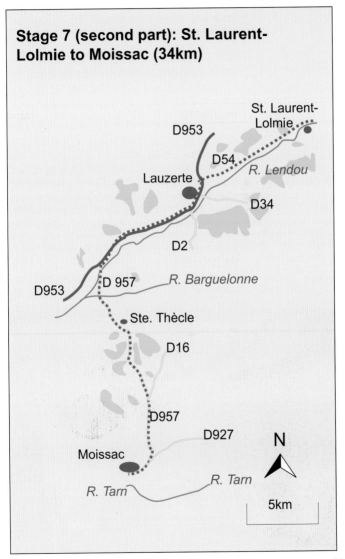

Stage 7 (second part): St. Laurent-Lolmie to Moissac (34km)

St Laurent-Lolmie 150m (384/1168)
Telephone.

After another easy 8km the D953 is met and joined (turn left). If you wish to see the town of Lauzerte, high on the hill above you, cross the D953 and climb steeply.

Lauzerte 280m (392/1160)
Gîte communal (06 19 70 89 49), Hotel du Quercy (05 63 94 66 36), chambre d'hôte (05 63 94 60 68), camping, bars, restaurants, shops and tourist office.
This beautiful medieval town, with its array of narrow streets, can be confusing. The Church of St Barthélémy should be seen. To return to the pilgrimage route, retrace your route as far as the D953 and turn right (southwest), signed Moissac and Valence.

If you do not wish to visit Lauzerte, then turn left onto the D953, leaving the town standing proudly above the road on the right. After 7km turn left onto the D957, signed to Moissac and Ste Thècle. Follow it until the River

Lauzerte – market square

Barguelonne is crossed twice. From the second bridge the road climbs steeply for 5km until it reaches the village of

Ste Thècle 182m (406/1146)
Bar, restaurant, shops and church.

Now the road descends, steepening gradually until after 6km the D16 joins it from the left (take care as vehicles joining from the left appear to have right of way), and after another 5km turn right, at the outskirts of Moissac, onto the D927. After a further kilometre, passing the ubiquitous supermarkets and building suppliers, this will lead you into the centre of

Moissac 76m (419/1133)
Twinned with Astorga, Moissac has four hotels, the Luxembourg (05 63 04 04 27), Le Chapon Fin (05 63 04 04 22), Recollets (05 63 04 25 44) and Le Port Napoleon (05 63 04 01 55). It also boasts a gîte d'étape (05 63 04 62 21) or accommodation at the Presbytère (05 63 04 02 81 or 05 63 04 01 44). There is a campsite, bars, restaurants, supermarket, banks and shops, including a cycle repair shop. In spite of all this, accommodation can be quite scarce and it is advisable to book your overnight stay as early as possible.
Moissac, sitting astride the River Tarn, is dominated by the Abbey of St Pierre, whose 13th-century tympanum, portal and 12th-century cloisters are breathtaking. Try to arrive here early so that time can be spent admiring the architecture.

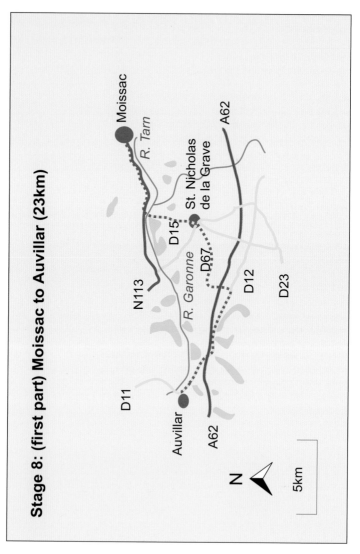

Stage 8: (first part) Moissac to Auvillar (23km)

STAGE 8
Moissac to Lectoure (59km)

Route	The hills return and there is quite a lot of awkward navigation in the vicinity of St Nicholas de la Grave and Auvillar. Study the map carefully before leaving.
Surfaces	Good all day.
See	The beautiful old market town of Auvillar, the tiny walled village of StAntoine and the breathtaking views from Lectoure.

Leave **Moissac** in a westerly direction on the N113. This drab exit to the town keeps the River Tarn to its left as it climbs out of Moissac until, after 4km, the D15 to the left is taken. (Take care – this is an awkward junction if traffic is heavy and it may be easier to dismount.) This quickly leads to

St Nicholas de la Grave 79m (428/1124)
Bar, shops.
The church, which is often locked, has a tower with a strange hole through it which can be seen from afar.

Having doglegged round the church, almost any route south of St Nicholas will suffice. The D67 signed to Merles is the best, if it can be found. If not, the D15 signed to Caumont, Lavit and Le Pin should be followed until the road crosses the AutoRoute, and at the crossroads soon afterwards turn right onto the D12, which will pass a picnic place just before a sharp bend leading into

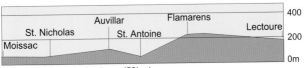

Stage 8: Moissac to Lectoure (59km)

Stage 8: (second part) Auvillar to Lectoure (36km)

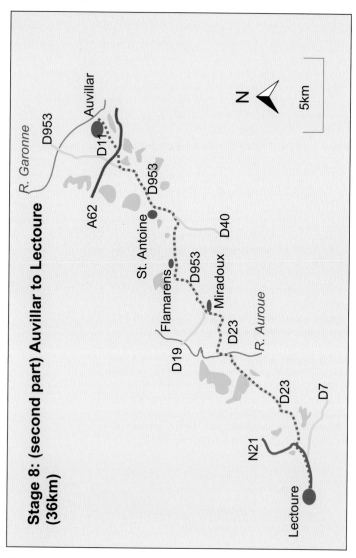

Auvillar 108m (442/1110)

Hotel de l'Horloge (05 63 39 91 61), gîte d'étape (05 63 39 57 33 or 05 63 39 89 82), two chambres d'hôte (05 63 39 62 45 and 05 67 79 77 97), restaurants, bars, shops and tourist office.

This is a beautiful old town of Roman origin which has been heavily though tastefully restored. Its market hall is quite magnificent, as are the views of the Garonne valley from the panorama. Visit the 12th-century Church of St Pierre, formerly a Benedictine monastery, and the Romanesque Chapelle Ste-Catherine, as well as the 17th-century clock tower close to numerous 16th-century wooden houses.

St Nicholas de la Grave – the church with the hole!

Turn left here onto the D11, signed Bardigues and Mansonville, which does not look too promising. At the junction at the top of the next hill, bear right onto the D88, signed to St Antoine. Cross the AutoRoute and ride parallel to it before slipping left onto the D953. At the first Y junction bear right, staying on the D953 to ride 3km into

St Antoine 63m (449/1103)

The last house in the village is still a gîte d'étape providing meals (05 62 28 64 27), but there are no shops.

This is a simple medieval gem – a walled village which was the site of an ancient pilgrim hospital and commanderie.

The D953 is now followed, signed to Miradoux and Lectoure (take care at road junctions), as it undulates and climbs steeply across open countryside before ascending the long steep hill into

Flamarens 211m (458/1094)

Water, toilets and telephone at the mairie.

The 13th-century castle would be worth a visit, but opening times are very limited.

Once through this picturesque but almost deserted village the road continues its switchback ride until, after another steep ascent, you fork left on the D953 for Miradoux and Lectoure. There are superb views along this stretch as the road makes a series of winding ascents and descents until it reaches

Miradoux 222m (462/1090)
Some pilgrim accommodation (05 62 28 66 57), bar, rooms at the bar, shops, bank with ATM, post office and pharmacy.
Visit the Gothic church with its ruined tower.

Continue on the D953 through the centre of the village, signed Lectoure, then beyond the village go right onto the D23, still signed to Lectoure, and gradually descend for 6km until the River Auroue is crossed. Continue on the D23 through the hamlet of Castet-Arrou (gîte d'étape and telephone) and for the next 7km climb and descend as the road crosses pleasant farmland before reaching the N21, 3km from Lectoure. Turn left onto this road, signed Auch, and make the last ascent of the day into the town centre.

Lectoure 186m (478/1074)
Hotel Relais St Jacques (05 62 68 83 79), four chambres d'hôtes, (05 62 68 81 56, 05 62 68 71 24, 05 62 68 82 63 and 05 62 68 71 27), as well as an excellent office de tourisme and a modern if somewhat depressing (no windows in the bedrooms) gîte d'étape with indoor bike storage – key at the tourist office (05 62 68 76 98) – bars, restaurants, banks and shops. There may also be some accommodation at the presbytery and the Soeurs de la Providence.
Lectoure, a town of Roman origin, is built on a bluff of land overlooking the valley of the Gers. The 13th-century Cathedral of St Gervais and St Portais is well worth a visit, and a stroll along the high promenade above the valley to take in the panorama is highly recommended.

Stage 9: (first part) Lectoure to Condom (22km)

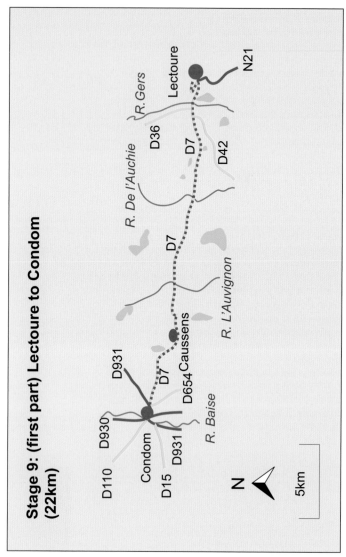

STAGE 9
Lectoure to Eauze (52km)

Route	A hilly stage with less climbing towards the end.
Surfaces	Good throughout.
See	The cathedral and museums in Condom, the walled village of Larressingle and the ancient *bastide* of Montréal

Leave Lectoure on the N21 down the main street in a westerly direction. Turn right onto the D7, signed Condom, descending for 2km in a sweeping arc with fine views below the town, before crossing the River Gers. It is worth looking back at Lectoure at this point to see how well defended it is on its rocky promontory.

Now begins an arduous ride due west on the D7, with a series of hills each approximately 1km up, the same down, and about 0.5km between each one. The countryside is pleasant if not spectacular, with most of the agricultural land given over to growing sunflowers or arable crops. There is no town or village for about 15km and little in the way of shelter. If you want a drink on the way, make sure your water bottles are full before you leave Lectoure, as there is no bar before you reach Caussens. The steepest hills are early in the journey, but the general impression is of an endless succession of climbs until reaching the hilltop village of

Caussens 203m 494/1058)
Roadside bar and restaurant.

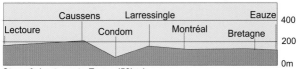

Stage 9: Lectoure to Eauze (52km)

Stage 9: (second part) Condom to Eauze (30km)

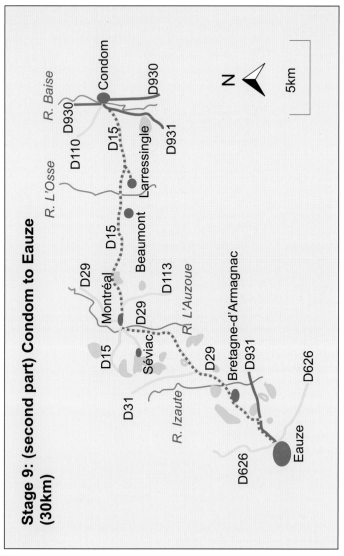

The final 6km into Condom are still hilly, but the gradients are not as severe as those encountered earlier in the stage until a final sharp climb through narrow streets brings you into the centre of this ancient town.

Condom 81m (500/1052)

Three hotels, Relais de la Ténarèze (05 62 28 02 54), the Hotel des Trois Lys (05 62 28 33 33) and the Hotel des Cordeliers (05 62 28 03 68), and two gîtes d'étapes (06 13 28 52 66 and 06 84 32 30 01). There is also a campsite, bars and restaurants, supermarket, banks, shops, a cycle shop, as well as a good office de tourisme (05 62 28 00 80).
The Gascon market town of Condom is built on a hill with the River Baise flowing along its western side. It has flourished as one of the chief centres of the Armagnac distribution industry and has a museum celebrating this fact. The main square, with its towering, flamboyant 16th-century Gothic Cathedral of St Pierre, built on the site of an 11th-century monastery, is at the highest point, with narrow medieval streets, many of which are pedestrianised, radiating from it. In recent years the town has also opened a new museum dedicated to the preservatif!

Leave Condom, following signs to Eauze, by crossing the river and taking the D15 signed for Montréal. At the roundabout take a right turn towards Larressingle. The hilly nature of the terrain continues. After 5km take a left turn, well signed, to Larressingle. This is a detour of 3km and the route from the main road you have just left has to be retraced. Climb very steeply until this perfect medieval fortified village is reached.

Larressingle 177m (507/1045)

Accommodation and meals at Auberge de Larressingle (05 62 28 29 67) and a gîte d'étape (06 62 77 29 72).
Only pedestrians and cyclists are allowed over the drawbridge to view this incredible gem of a fortified walled 13th-century village, with church, castle, bar and souvenir shops. In high season it can be packed with tourists, but on a quiet day it has a remarkable atmosphere.

Larressingle – the walled village

Return to the D15 and continue to climb and descend at regular intervals. After 3km it appears from the signs that Château Beaumont is a bus shelter on the left! Just beyond it, do not take the D254 to the left, sign-posted Lauraët, but continue along the D15 into the quaint bastide (defended and fortified) town of

Montréal du Gers 135m (515/1037)
Hotel St Jacques (05 62 29 43 07), restaurants and bars, shops, tourist office, post office.

Although not perfect in form, Montréal du Gers is built on the site of a prehistoric hill fort, and this interesting 13th-century bastide is as good as you are likely to see on the whole route.

Leave Montréal due south on the D29. Close to here are signs to the Roman villa at **Séviac**. If time allows this is worth visiting for its spectacular mosaic floors. (Chambre d'hôte, 05 62 29 44 12, next door.) Return to the D29. The road continues to undulate. Ignore roads to the right and left close to **Lamothe** but continue on the D29 for another 4km into

Bretagne-d'Armagnac 151m (528/1024)
Bar and restaurant.
This rather windswept village is one of those producing the world-famous Armagnac, whose centres of distribution are Condom, Eauze and Aire-sur-L'Adour.

Continue along the D29 for another 3km and then turn right onto the D931, which in another 3km leads directly into

Eauze 142m (530/1022)
Eauze is a small market town with hotels which may be closed, restaurants, bars, post office, banks, supermarket and shops, including a cycle shop. Close to the town centre there is a basic gîte d'étape opposite the office de tourisme (05 62 09 85 62 or 06 85 17 65 15), where the key is lodged. There is a summer campsite here.
The town dates back to Roman times and has an excellent museum of Roman artefacts. The 15th-century Gothic Cathedral of St Luperc is worth a visit and there are several attractive half-timbered houses.

Stage 10: (first part) Eauze to Nogaro (19km)

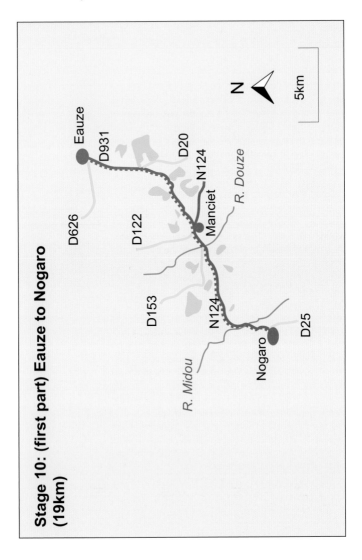

STAGE 10
Eauze to Pimbo (63km)

Route	The first portion of the stage is easy and pleasant, but after Aire sur L'Adour the route becomes very hilly.
Surfaces	Good.
See	Church of Ste Quitterie in Aire sur L'Adour and the ancient pilgrim church in Pimbo.
Warning	Accommodation is very limited on this stage and it is worth ringing ahead to confirm there are places to be had.

Take the D931 south out of Eauze, signposted Nogaro. This excellent quiet road has none of the harsh hills encountered in previous days and the surface is almost perfect for cycling. In 9km cross the railway at

Manciet 120m (540/1012)
Hotels, bars, excellent auberge with rooms, gîtes d'étapes (06 68 87 78 24 and 06 73 32 50 79), office de tourisme (05 62 08 50 01) and shops.
This 11th-century walled town built around its château used to have a 12th-century Templars' commanderie.

The main road now becomes the N124 and maintains its good condition. Although there are several hills, the gradients are far easier than previously encountered, and 9km further on is the market town of

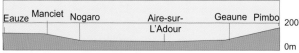
Stage 10: Eauze to Pimbo (63km)

Stage 10: (second part) Nogaro to Pimbo (44km)

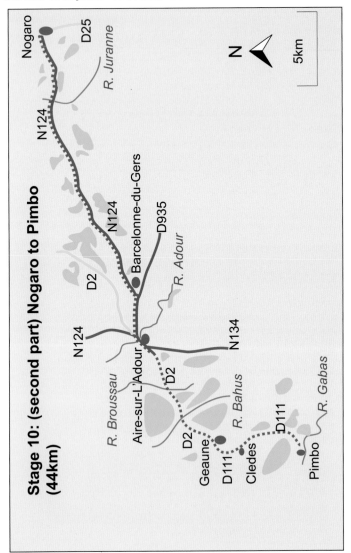

Nogaro 98m (549/1003)

Hotels – Solenca (05 62 09 09 08), le Commerce (05 62 09 00 95) and Les Arènes (05 62 09 03 33) – gîte d'étape (05 62 69 06 15), campsite, bars, restaurants, supermarket, tourist office, post office and shops. Spar open Sunday mornings even during bank holiday weekends.

The 11th-century Church of St Nicholas, at the far end of the town close to the remains of a pilgrim hospital, is worth a visit to see the recently restored frescoes.

The N124 should now be followed for the next 21km into the centre of Aire sur L'Adour. The way is not too hilly and has an excellent surface, but it does not pass through any town or village of note until it reaches Barcelonne-du-Gers, an uninspiring out-of-town retail area 4km from Aire-sur-L'Adour. Ride from here directly into the centre of

Aire-sur-L'Adour 81m (570/982)

Hotel de la Paix (05 58 71 60 70) has a special tariff for pilgrims, Chez l'Ahumat (05 58 71 82 61) has rooms. There is a gîte d'étape in the Centre de Loisir (05 58 03 26 22), several chambres d'hôte (05 58 71 63 03), a campsite, bars and restaurants, as well as shops, a cycle shop and a supermarket.

Aire-sur-L'Adour, which is entered over the main river bridge, is a bustling market town which rewards those who stay to explore it. The 12th-century cathedral is rather sombre, but the Church of Ste Quitterie du Mas in the upper part of the town is fascinating, especially the crypt, with its 4th-century sarcophagus. The keys (and a guided tour) are available from a few doors away. It is an experience that should not be missed.

Now begins the most arduous section of the stage. Leave Aire-sur-L'Adour on the N134 by the steep hill which passes the end of the road leading to the church of Ste Quitterie. Once clear of the outskirts of the town, turn right at a roundabout onto the D2, signed for Geaune, which will be reached in 13km.

Pimbo – a medieval village

Geaune 90m (583/969)

Bar and helpful Hotel de Ville for accommodation. Two beds may be available in the Centre Parroissial (05 58 44 51 82).

Here take the left turn on the D111, signed to Cledes (telephone). Having passed through Cledes the road surface is poor, but will bring you, after yet another strenuous climb, into

Pimbo 190m (593/959)

Bar, gîte communal (05 58 44 46 57 or 05 58 44 49 18) and possible chambre d'hôte (05 58 44 49 23 or 05 58 44 46 92) in this quiet, ancient bastide, with a helpful pilgrim welcome in the Salle des Fêtes. Drinking water available outside the mairie, which may also be able to provide rooms.

The collegiate Church of St Barthélémy has some beautiful and very interesting decoration both inside and out. There has been a monastery here since the 8th-century. During the 12th century the bastide, the oldest in the Landes, fell into English hands and was not restored to French rule for 400 years.

STAGE 11
Pimbo to Navarrenx (62km)

Route	An arduous ride on winding roads.
Surfaces	Generally good, but first 20km may be rough.
See	The ancient abbey at Le Sauvelade.
Warning	The majority of the route is on minor roads which are difficult to follow and not well signed.

Take a left turn at Pimbo on the D111, signed Arzacq, and follow the road to Boucoue. Turn left here and the road becomes the D32, then the D946, leading to

Arzacq-Arraziguet 231m (599/953)
Hotel la Vieille Auberge (05 59 04 51 31), gîte d'étape and campsite in Centre d'Accueil (05 59 04 41 41). The bar/café may be closed at lunchtime. There is a restaurant, bank with ATM and shops.
Small country towns such as this have little to detain the pilgrim, and seem at times to be deserted. This one has two squares, neither of which seems necessary – they are probably the remains of the English bastide built in the 14th century.

Leave the wide town square of Arzacq on the D946 left, heading across country for Morlanne and Orthez. The latter part of this extremely hilly road is virtually deserted, with few houses or farms in sight, but the Pyrenees come clearly into view.

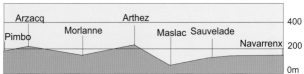

Stage 11: Pimbo to Navarrenx (62km)

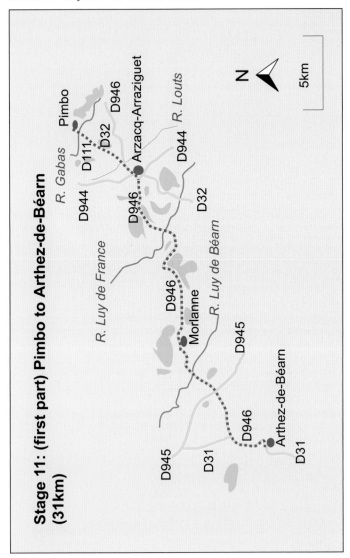

Stage 11: (first part) Pimbo to Arthez-de-Béarn (31km)

Morlanne 148m (613/939)

Chambre d'hôte (05 59 81 47 98), ferme auberge, post office, tourist office.

The well-decorated exterior of the fortified church is interesting, but the bulding may be locked, and the 14th-century château may not yet be open after extensive restoration work.

Continue on the D946 for 8km, crossing the D945 and following signs for Arthez until you reach a T-junction with the D31. Turn left and climb the very steep hill into

Arthez-de-Béarn 211m (624/928)

Here there are bars, restaurants, campsite, simple gîte d'étape (05 59 67 70 52), chambres d'hôtes beyond the town, a cycle shop, bank with ATM and a small supermarket, but no hotel.

Do not miss the Chapelle de Caubin, the ancient commanderie of the Knights of Saint John.

The exit from Arthez-de-Béarn is not obvious. At the top of the hill take a narrow right-hand road for Mesplede and Orthez, but at the next junction bear left, signed to the Gendarmerie. This is the D275 and it begins a long descent from Arthez to the N117. At the junction with the N117 turn right and ride along it for 100m before turning left onto the D275, signed Maslacq, to cross the River Gave and the AutoRoute into

Maslacq 79m (632/920)

Expensive Hotel Maugouber (05 59 38 78 00), bar, gîte d'étape (05 59 67 60 79), tourist office and shops.

Do not take the D9 out of Maslacq but continue on a minor road, the D275, signed Sapourenx and Orthez, and at the next junction turn left for Sauvelade. After approximately 5km turn left at a T-junction onto the D110 and follow this road for a couple kilometres into the tiny hamlet of

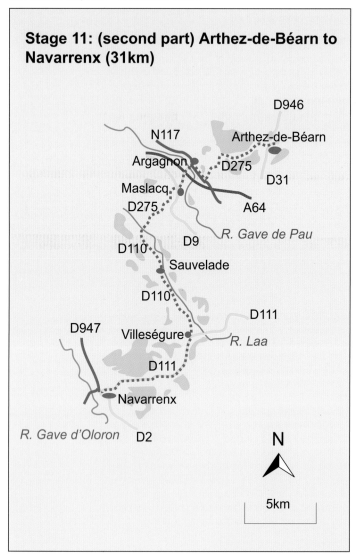

Stage 11: (second part) Arthez-de-Béarn to Navarrenx (31km)

Sauvelade 110m (641/911)

Modern gîte d'étape (05 59 67 33 69 or 07 85 65 87 59) in an ancient abbey – it takes block bookings so could be full. Newly opened bar/café and simple grocery store. Chambre d'hôte may be available in the village (05 59 67 60 57). There is a water tap and telephone.

Most interesting 12th-century Benedictine and, later, Cistercian abbey, and rather austere13th-century church of St Jacques, which was visited by King Edward 1 of England and his queen to celebrate the 17th anniversary of his coronation.

On leaving Sauvelade bear left onto the D110, and after 5km turn right and follow the signs on this valley road into the village of

Villeségure 121m (646/906)

Shops, telephone, post office and small office de tourisme.

Ride through the centre, turn left and right, signed Navarrenx, and descend steeply to the D111. Here turn

Sauvelade – the ancient abbey

95

Navarrenx –
the arsenal

right onto this wide, well-surfaced road, heading for Navarrenx, which you will reach in 9km after a series of stiff climbs.

Navarrenx 125m (655/897)

Contact the bar in the town square (Le Dahu) for the gîte communal (05 59 66 02 67) which is to be found in the ancient arsenal. A second gîte d'étape (05 59 66 07 25) can be found on the outskirts of the town. There is also a basic campsite and a cycle shop. An interesting 14th-century walled medieval bastide town with hotels, bars, shops, a supermarket, and a tourist office that will stamp your pilgrim passport and provide an excellent plan of the town. On market days the centre of Navarrenx can become very congested.

STAGE 12
Navarrenx to St-Jean-Pied-de-Port (61km)

Route	This feels like a long tiring stage with steep hills. Traffic can be heavy in the latter portion of the journey.
Surfaces	Generally good, but the first few kilometres and the stretch around Harambeltz may be poor.
See	Harambeltz church and the pilgrim villages of Ostabat and St Jean-Pied- de-Port.

Turn left on the D947. Cross the River Gave d'Oloron, and once over the bridge turn immediately right on the D115 for **Castelnau-Camblong**, which is reached in a kilometre. Then take the D115 for Nabas. The badly surfaced road again climbs and falls rapidly through wooded scenery for 11km before dropping to cross the main road, the River Saison and the railway to enter

Nabas 90m (668/884)
telephone,

on the D23. The D23 continues for 2km to cross more undulating country (you are now in the foothills of the Pyrenees), then turn right onto the D115, signed to Aroue and St Palais, until it reaches

Aroue 125m (674/878)
A prosperous little village including a gîte d'étape (05 59 65 95 54) and a shop.

Stage 12: Navarrenx to St.-Jean-Pied-de-Port (61km)

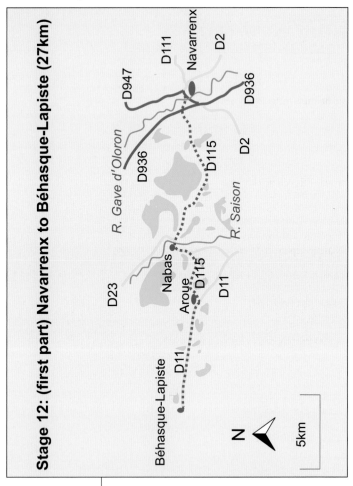

Stage 12: (first part) Navarrenx to Béhasque-Lapiste (27km)

There is an interesting church dedicated to St Etienne in which can be found a statue of St Jacques Matamoros (the Moor-slayer) – rarely seen in France but very common in Spain – as part of a bas-relief, although the church may be closed.

Turn right here onto the D11, signed St Palais. In a kilometre, on the right, a small garage sells drinks, etc., and is very sympathetic to pilgrims, offering its shady trees as a picnic spot. It also holds the key for the local gîte d'étape. Another 8km along the constantly undulating D11, having passed through the villages of **Etcharry**, **Domezain** and **Berraute**, enter the village of

Béhasque-Lapiste 122m (682/870)
Telephone.

Look out for a minor road, the C1, past the church to the left. This will quickly lead you onto the newly made D933, with cycle lane, which crosses the River Bidouze. At the roundabout turn left onto the D933, heading for St-Jean-Pied-de-Port.

If you wish to visit St Palais, ignore the turn in Béhasque-Lapiste and continue along the D11. (Do not take the road that drops steeply to the right as you enter the town).

Harambeltz – the ancient pilgrim chapel

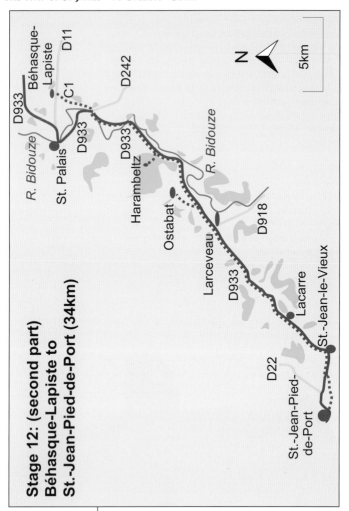

Stage 12: (second part)
Béhasque-Lapiste to
St.-Jean-Pied-de-Port (34km)

St Palais 125m
Many hotels, bars, restaurants, shops, a cycle shop, tourist office and supermarket. Pilgrims can also be accommodated

at the very welcoming *Communauté Franciscaine, 1 Ave de Gibraltar (05 59 65 90 77)*, on the outskirts of the town, heading towards St-Jean-Pied-de-Port.

This is a very busy 12th-century market town with a strong Spanish influence. You may be tempted to leave St Palais by way of the D302 to see the Stele de Gibraltar, where the paths from Le Puy, Vezelay and Paris meet, but if the gradient is too daunting take the D933 out of the town and whisk along its smooth level surface, keeping the River Bidouze alongside.

The route from Béhasque-Lapiste joins from the left 4km along this road.

After 6km of enjoyable riding you can take a right-hand turn to Harambeltz to see the strange, isolated 11th-century chapel/pilgrim hospital dedicated to St Nicholas, but you must return to the D933 by the same route. The same goes for visiting

Ostabat-Asme 124m (695/857)

Gîtes d'étapes Aire Ona (05 59 37 88 75 or 06 33 65 77 15) and Izarrak (just out of village, 05 59 37 81 10 or 06 72 73 78 56), cultural centre, café, chambre d'hôte (05 59 37 85 03), bar, restaurant and shops.

Ostabat-Asme

This beautiful 12th-century village nestling in the foot-hills of the Pyrenees was once much bigger, providing for hordes of pilgrims who descended on its hospices and hospitals every day. Evidence of some of its former glory can be seen in nearby ruins. There used to be two roads into this hilltop village, but recent roadworks seem to have closed the first, and it may be necessary to take the second road and ride back into the village, returning by the same road. It adds no more than 2km to the day's journey.

Having passed the junction with the D918 where the cycle lane ends at

Larceveau 160m (699/853)
two hotels – Espellet (05 59 37 81 91) and Trinquet (05 59 37 81 59) – bars, restaurants, pharmacy and shops to the left of the main road,

the cycle lane is reinstated and the road begins to climb and descend as it approaches the Pyrenees proper, but there is nothing too steep anywhere on this stage. Soon you will pass

Lacarre 234m (707/845)
Bar and restaurant, but nothing else to detain you.

The road tends to be busier now, especially in the holiday season. The next village to be encountered is

St Jean-le-Vieux 212m (711/841)
Hotel Mendy (05 59 37 11 81), less busy than in St Jean-Pied-de-Port and generally cheaper, chambres d'hôtes (06 86 99 82 03), restaurants, shops and camping.
This was a Roman town, founded in the first century as the Roman camp confirms. Do not miss the fine Gothic doorway of the Church of the Madeleine.

Leave the village and after 2km turn left off the D933 onto an unsigned country lane to La Magdeleine. Having passed through the village, climb very steeply to the citadel overlooking St-Jean-Pied-de-Port and bear right to enter the town through the pilgrim gate, the Porte Saint-Jacques. This road is cobbled and it is advisable to dismount before descending the steep Rue de la Citadelle.

St-Jean-Pied-de-Port 180m (716/836)

St-Jean-Pied-de-Port is a busy tourist town with shops including a cycle repair shop, supermarket, tourist office, hotels, camping, restaurants and bars, and several houses along the Rue de la Citadelle advertising beds at low prices. Have your pilgrim passport stamped at the pilgrim office in the Rue de la Citadelle. It will also furnish you with all the relevant information for the rest of your journey. There is an office de tourisme (05 59 37 03 57) and three gîtes d'étapes in the town (05 59 49 10 86, 05 24 34 19 00 and 05 59 37 24 68).

The citadel, built in 1688, is worth visiting for its views of the Pyrenees and the following day's route. The 14th-century Gothic Church of St Jean is also interesting.

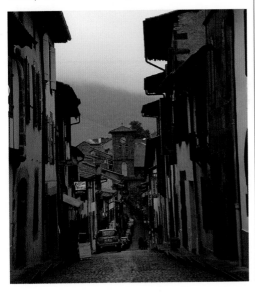

*St Jean-Pied-de-Port –
the Rue de la Citadelle*

STAGE 13
St-Jean-Pied-de-Port to Burguete (40km)

Route	This is a short day in terms of distance, but it does include a lot of climbing. It is the longest climb of the pilgrimage so far, but do not be put off by horror stories. Much of the early part of the route is easy and there is plenty of shade if it is hot. There are lots of resting points and an ample supply of water.
Surfaces	Good throughout.
See	The monastery and treasures at Roncesvalles.
Warning	Watch out for large, nasty horse flies on the ascent. The refuge in Roncesvalles could be overcrowded, if not full.

Leave St-Jean-Pied-de-Port by the D933, clearly signed to Pamplona, Roncesvalles and Spain – there are chambres d'hôtes along this stretch of road. This begins as a pleasant ride through rolling wooded hills with the river to your right. The road rises gently and the ascent is no problem at all. The village of

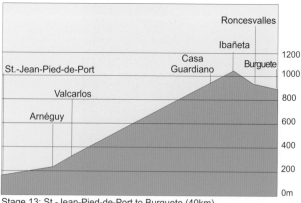

Stage 13: St.-Jean-Pied-de-Port to Burguete (40km)

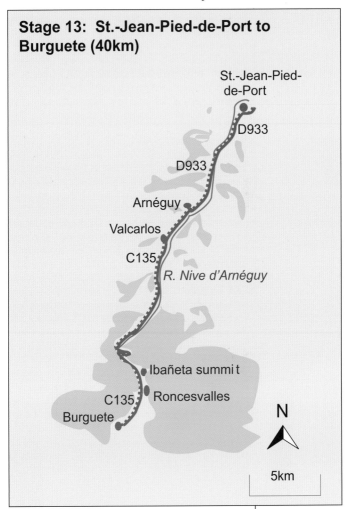

Stage 13: St.-Jean-Pied-de-Port to Burguete (40km)

St.-Jean-Pied-de-Port

D933

D933

Arnéguy

Valcarlos

C135

R. Nive d'Arnéguy

Ibañeta summit

Roncesvalles

C135

Burguete

N

5km

Arnéguy 245m (724/828)
bars, hotel, restaurant and shops but little else of interest,

is passed through, and shortly afterwards a sign at the redundant customs post informs you that you have now entered Spain. Remember to extend a greeting to oncoming cyclists now of 'Hola' rather than 'Bonjour'! From here the road, which has now become the N135, begins to climb more steeply, but never becomes truly daunting. The surface is good and there is little heavy traffic apart from the odd timber truck. Another 3km will see you in

Valcarlos 320m (727/825)
Hotel, two hostals, casa rural, chambres d'hôtes, bars, restaurants and shops.
Santiago Matamoros makes an appearance in the church.

It is from here that the climb really begins. The gradients are consistently steep for the next 17km, with no villages and a road surface that may be poor in places. If there is low cloud, which is very common here, remember to switch on your lights – motorists take many of the hairpin bends at speed and may not see you. On reaching Casa Guardiano, 3km before the summit, the gradient increases and this last stretch is an unrelenting drag with your goal, the chapel at the top of the Ibañeta Pass, visible high up in front of you.

Ibañeta summit 1057m (750/802)
The top of the pass is worth visiting, if only to recuperate for a few minutes. In cold weather, put on warm clothing before muscles stiffen. The chapel was built in 1965 and has a bell to guide in pilgrims in low cloud. It is often closed, but the mound of crosses left by grateful pilgrims is visible to the right of it, as is the monument to Roland, commander of Charlemagne's army, who according to legend met his fate hereabouts (probably ambushed by marauding Basques). On a clear day the views are superb.

There is now a short descent to

Roncesvalles 952m (753/799)
Here there is accommodation in the refuge opposite the

monastery or at one of the two hostals, *Casa Sabina (948 76 00 12)* or *La Posada (948 76 02 25)*, which also serves meals *(you must book a table in advance)*. There are no food shops. The refuge does not open until 4.00pm but it is wise to arrive early and queue if you want a bed for the night, as large numbers of pilgrims arrive by bus from Pamplona and all expect to find accommodation here.

It is worth a visit to the 13th-century Augustinian monastery and hospital, with its fine treasury but rather strange zinc roof, which is being replaced. A new museum is beautifully organised and has helpful multilingual staff.

Take the C135 from Roncesvalles towards Pamplona. This is a good, generally well-surfaced road which descends gently for 3km to the Basque village of

Burguete 893m (756/796)
Hostal Jaundeaburre (948 760078), *Hotel Burguete (948 760005)* and *Hotel Loizu*, rooms, bars, restaurants, bank, small supermarket and pharmacy.
Some fine 18th-century houses can be seen lining the main street.

The Ibañeta Pass – typical weather

Roncesvalles –inside the church

STAGE 14
Burguete to Puente la Reina (74km)

Route	Quite a toil as far as Zubiri, but afterwards the riding is easy until Pamplona has been left behind.
Surfaces	Generally good, but unsurfaced near Eunate.
See	All the sights of Pamplona, the tiny church of Eunate and the medieval town of Puente la Reina.
Warning	Spanish drivers tend to give cyclists less room than the French. The exit from Pamplona can be very confusing.

The road continues its gentle descent for another 2km, at which point it swings sharply to the right 1km before the ancient Basque village of

Espinal 871m (760/792)
Campsite, rooms, bars, restaurants, shops, small super-market and doctor.
Look out for the coats of arms over the doorways in this 13th-century Basque village.

Stay on the N135 signed to Pamplona. Now begins 12km of ascent and descent with a series of hairpin bends until you reach the two villages of

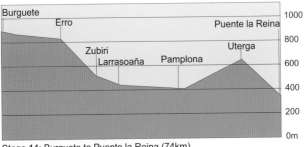

Stage 14: Burguete to Puente la Reina (74km)

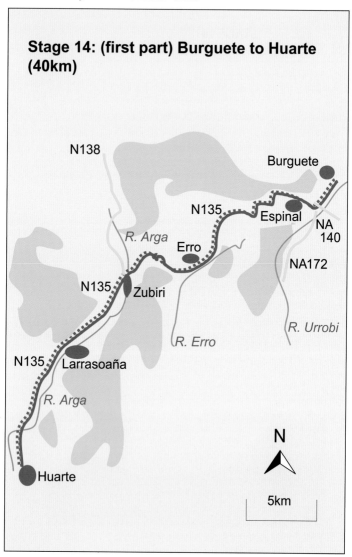

Stage 14: (first part) Burguete to Huarte (40km)

Gerendiain 866m (768/784)
casa rural, bar and restaurant
and

Erro 801m (772/780)
bank, pharmacy and bread shop.

There is now a short ascent to

Alto d'Erro 810m (776/776)
No facilities, but the views from here are very good in clear weather.

Continue on the N135 as it begins a sharp winding descent until it reaches

Zubiri 526m (782/770)
Refuge, Hostal Gau Txori (948 30 45 31), Hosteria de Zubiri (948 30 43 29), bar, restaurant, shop and bank.
This grey, depressing little Basque town has nothing to detain the pilgrim except the former hospital building immediately before the medieval bridge across the River Arga.

Continue down the valley, keeping the river to your left. Ride into and pause at the small town of

Larrasoaña 450m (789/763)
Refugio for walkers (no cyclists allowed), pension and bar.
The mayor is very supportive of pilgrims and will be keen to stamp your pilgrim passport and show you his collection of camino memorabilia. The restored medieval bridge is worth a look, as is the church with its statue of Santiago.
The downhill gradient is now gentle as the valley widens, and in 10km, before the town of Huarte appears, turn right at the interchange with the new road system, heading for Pamplona on the NA32. Avoid Huarte town centre, but keep following signs to Pamplona on the N135. This road continues through the suburbs of Pamplona with a cycle lane alongside until it reaches the centre of

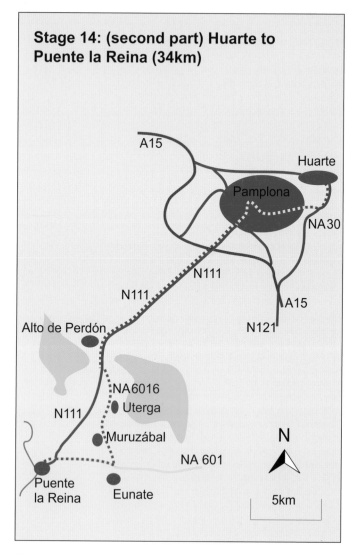

Stage 14: (second part) Huarte to Puente la Reina (34km)

Pamplona 415m (806/746)

All facilities are available, including a post office and several cycle repair shops, although there is a refuge that refuses to accept pilgrims on bikes. Hotel accommodation is bookable through the tourist office, but can be expensive (disproportionately so during the San Fermin – running of the bulls – festival). The Hotel Bearán (948 223428) in the Calle San Nicolas is reasonable and has secure bicycle storage and a lift.

Pamplona is difficult to negotiate even with a street map (available from the tourist office – if you can find it, tucked away in the Calle Anumada). There are many one-way streets, and a number of intersecting medieval streets that can be explored – the best way to see the city is on foot. Restaurants and bars are plentiful and can be very good value. The 14th-century Gothic cathedral, especially the cloisters, should be visited – they will put a stamp (sello) in your pilgrim passport. See also the churches of San Sernin, San Domingo, San Nicholás and San Lorenzo.

The route out of Pamplona is very difficult to find. The town plan available from the tourist office should help, but you may have to ask for directions as you go along. From the city centre, look for signs for Logroño or Estella on the N111. Swing left around the far side of the park onto the Avenida Pio XII. Continue straight on this road through numerous sets of traffic lights with more signs to Logroño. Head out of the city following signs for Estella and Logroño on the N111. Once the Autovia (A15) has been crossed the route is obvious, although road improvements may mean that cyclists will not be allowed to ride on this stretch in future, in which case information needs to be obtained from Pamplona tourist office.

Leave **Cizur Mayor** (two refuges) on your right (there is no need to visit this village unless you are seeking refuge accommodation) and cycle towards the line of wind turbines you can see stretched out on a hilltop to your left and in front of you. At present the N111 here is wide and has a good cycle lane, and although traffic is fast it is not heavy, and the road surface is good. The road climbs

113

steadily until the **Alto de Perdón** (780m) is reached in 10km. Here there are stupendous views of the rest of the day's journey. About 1km after the top, slip right to cross the N111 onto a new country road, the NA6016, heading for

Uterga 650m (823/729)
Tiny refuge, casa rural, restaurant, cold drinks machine, fountain and bar – which may be closed.
Another couple of kilometres further on the village of **Muruzábal** (bar) will be reached. Here take a good track (not tarmac) to the left, signed for Eunate. This sweeps through farmland until it reaches the main road opposite

Eunate church 680m (826/726)
This absolutely stunning 12th-century Romanesque church (closed Mondays), sitting in splendid isolation and dedicated to Santa Maria, should not be missed. It was probably a funeral chapel with a surrounding octagonal

Eunate – approaching the church

cloister, although the funeral lantern has been replaced by a small bell tower. There is a visitors' centre here, but it may not be open.

Alternatively, take the tarmac road out of Muruzábal until it reaches the main road and turn left, signed Campanas, until Eunate is reached. Having visited the church, turn left onto the NA601 road which joins the N111 1km short of Puente la Reina, at the point where the Pyrenean routes to Santiago all meet. This is marked with a modern statue of a walking pilgrim outside a modern hotel.

Puenta la Reina 346m (830/722)

Three refuges, hostal, hotels – Hotel Rural Bidean (948 34 04 57) – fondas, rooms, campsite, restaurants, bars and shops.

This is an interesting medieval market town with a famous 11th-century six-span bridge over the River Arga. The 12th-century Church of Santiago is worth a visit, if only to gaze at the wooden 14th-century polychrome statue of St Jacques which graces it. Before the bridge, visit the 15th-century church of St Pierre to see the statue of Notre Dame du Puy and, of course, one of Santiago. Alongside the Church of the Crucifixion is one of the oldest remaining pilgrims' hospices on the whole camino.

Puente la Reina – confluence of paths

STAGE 15
Puente la Reina to Viana (65km)

Route	A good but often exposed stage.
Surfaces	Good provided the main route is adhered to.
See	The church of San Pedro in Estella and the architecture of Viana.
Warning	If the weather is hot, the stretch from Estella to Viana can be exhausting.

Leave over the bridge, turning back onto the N111 signed for Estella. The road undulates a great deal but the surface is good, although major roadworks threaten to disrupt traffic for some time into the future. Traffic lanes are narrow with nowhere for cyclists to escape to. Most of the small hilltop towns and villages on this stretch, such as

Cirauqui (498m)
shops, restaurant and bars
12th-century Church of San Roman, plus a 13th-century church dedicated to Santa Catalina

Lorca (483m)
bar and shop
12th-century Church of Santa Maria

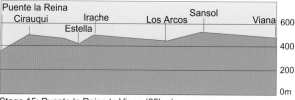

Stage 15: Puente la Reina to Viana (65km)

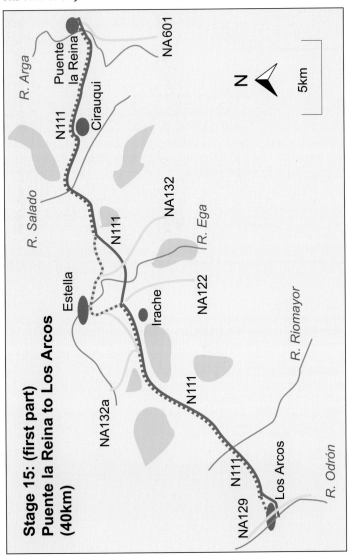

**Stage 15: (first part)
Puente la Reina to Los Arcos
(40km)**

Villatuerta (472m)
refugio, bar at sports hall
a *sello* can be obtained from 8 Plaza Iglesia, as can the
key to the 15th-century Church of the Asuncion

*Puente la Reina –
ancient pilgrim bridge*

are just off the main road and can be visited if necessary.
There is an air of dereliction hereabouts which was not
experienced on the French part of the way. The villages
seem deserted and do not attract the pilgrim except as
a relief from the N111. Farming seems to be a hit-and-
miss affair, with fields overgrown and untended, although
some terraces seem to be in process of being re-culti-
vated. After 19km the road dips and the NA122 is taken
for 3km to enter the town of

Estella 426m (849/703)
*Refuge, hotel, hostals, campsite, restaurants, bars, shops and
cycle repairs. Hostal San Andrés (948 554158) provides
adequate accommodation and bike storage and the Hostal
El Volante (948 55 39 57 or 638 02 90 05) has rooms.*
Although much of Estella is very ancient (11th century)
it is not particularly attractive. It has a large main square
with a busy market, but there is an air of sadness and

decay about the place. The 12th-century Palace of the Kings of Navarre, by the town hall (for your sello), is worth a visit. Compare the architecture of the Church of San Pedro de la Rua with that of San Miguel, whose doorway is stunning, on the other side of the river.

Leave Estella by the N111, signed Ayegui, and climb steadily through minor industrial buildings out of the town until on the left is seen the monastery of

Irache 500m (852/700)
Hotel, restaurant and café.
This 12th-century Benedictine monastery is worth visiting (free to pilgrims) – open Tuesday 9.30–13.30, Wednesday to Sunday 9.30–13.30 and 17.00–19.00. Alongside it is the famous wine fountain, where the local red may be available free of charge to pilgrims, as is cold water – the wine is potent stuff, so remember that you have a long hard ride still to come!

Irache – wine fountain

The road to Los Arcos and Logroño now climbs and drops over a none-too-inspiring countryside of scrub and wasteland, avoiding any place of interest for another 15km until a well-signed road to the right leaves the N111 and leads straight into the centre of

Los Arcos 447m (870/682)
Hostal Ezequiel (948 64 01 07 – pilgrim discount plus bike storage), Hotel Monaco (948 640000), rooms at Casa Alberde, refuges where cyclists may not be made to feel welcome, bar, pharmacy, restaurant and bank.
The town with its shady central square is now bypassed by the

main road. The flamboyant 12th-century Gothic Church of Santa María has an interesting cloister and choir stalls, and several houses on the main street boast coats of arms. It was here in former days that pilgrims changed their Navarrese money for that of Castille, no doubt to their disadvantage – no euros in those days!

Having taken a well-earned rest while exploring this little community, continue straight through the town and the N111 will be regained very shortly. This shadeless road now continues for another 7km until it reaches

Irache – entrance to the monastery

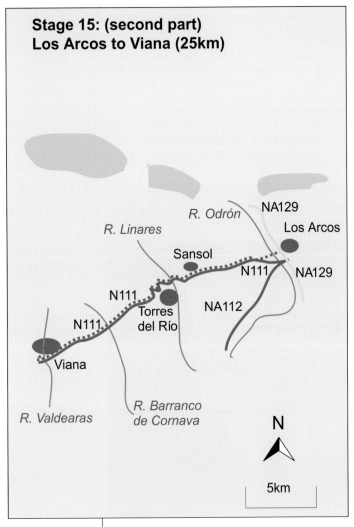

Stage 15: (second part)
Los Arcos to Viana (25km)

Sansol 505m (877/675)
Shop and pharmacy.

Leave the main road to visit the town. It has a fine church, dedicated to San Zoilo, with interesting frescoes. There is an excellent panorama from the front of the church.

Regain the main road as it sweeps down past the most attractive village of

Torres del Río 520m (879/673)
Refuge (private) and two bars.

Once again, leave the N111 to explore the village. Its 12th-century octagonal church dedicated to Saint-Sépulcre looks superb, but it may be locked. Built about 1200, it shows a mixture of styles from Romanesque to Gothic, with a distinct Mudéjar (Spanish Moorish) influence in its cupola.

Return to the N111 before climbing steeply via a series of hairpin bends over wild open moorland with little shade or shelter. Much of the land is still scrub, but some new planting has taken place on lower slopes. On reaching the summit an exhilarating descent leads, 16km later, to a turn to the right that leads into

Viana 466m (895/657)
The road climbs steeply in a wide sweep round the town before reaching the central square which one comes upon almost by surprise. The town has all facilities. There is a large, well-equipped refuge (948 645007) which welcomes cyclists and has secure storage for bikes. There are hotels – Palacio Pujadas (948 646464 for unashamed luxury), Hostal Casa Armendariz (948 645078) – bars, restaurants and shops, most of which are to be found on the Calle Mayor, the main street.

The 15th-century Church of Santa María, outside which Cesar Borgia is buried, is very large and very fine. Many houses along the Calle Mayor are decorated with armorial bearings. At one end of the main street is a primitive bullring where aspiring youths practice a non-lethal version of the 'sport'. From the ruined church and park of San Pedro, alongside the refuge, there is an excellent view across the plain to Logroño.

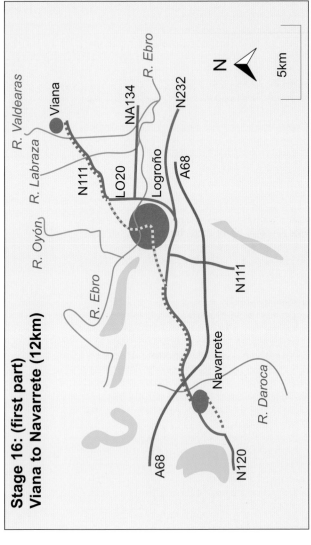

STAGE 16
Viana to Santo Domingo de la Calzada (49km)

Route	In general the route follows the N120, a busy but excellent trunk road. However, the city of Logroño has to be negotiated and this could cause a problem.
Surfaces	Excellent throughout.
See	Santa Maria cathedral in Logroño, the cloisters at the monastery of Santa Maria la Real in Nájera, the church and the hencoop at Santo Domingo de la Calzada.

The descent from Viana to the main N111 is very fine, with good views over Logroño and of the route to come. The road is wide with an excellent cycle lane and soon becomes the Logroño ring road, the LO20. This road is of motorway standard with attendant crash barriers, flyovers and tunnels. You may not wish to ride on it at all, in which case turn right into the city centre to visit

Logroño 384m (901/651)
Refuge (941 26 02 34 or 941 23 92 01), many hotels and hostals, fonda, campsite, post office, shops including cycle repairs, banks, bars and restaurant. Ask at the tourist office for a map and their recommendation for a route for cyclists heading out of the city in the direction of Navarrete, reminding them that cyclists should not ride on motorways.

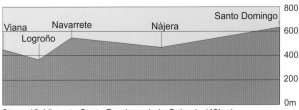

Stage 16: Viana to Santo Domingo de la Calzada (49km)

The churches of San Bartolomé, Santa María de Palacio and the famous Santiago with its statue of Santiago Matamoros can all be visited, as can the fine cathedral of Santa María Redonda, and the Museo de la Rioja next to the post office.

At present it appears that you will need to return to the LO20 to leave the city. Extreme care should be taken if you need to ride on or cross this road – it is not recommended. It may be advisable to become a walker and push your bike until you reach Navarrete. In this case leave by the Barriocepo, Puerta del Revellin, Comandancia, Trinidad, Gonzalo de Berceo, Superundia, Marqués de Murrieta, and turn left at the first petrol station. Whichever road you take, head west for Burgos, which may be signed A12 or N120. At the A12/N120 junction, keep to the right-hand lane signed the N120 to Navarrete. Follow this and it will quickly lead you to an awkward turning to the left into Navarrete. Do not turn onto the A68 as you are not allowed on this motorway with a bicycle.

Navarrete 555m (907/645)
Refuge (cyclists may be turned away), Hostal la Carrioca (941 440006), campsite, shops, restaurants, bank and bars. Navarrete has a fine 16th-century church with an incredible Baroque reredos which should not be missed. The town is famous for its pottery, made from the rich red clay found hereabouts. This is the last place of any significance before Nájera, so it would be wise to purchase food and drinks before continuing.

The main street of Navarrete quickly leads back onto the N120, which is now slavishly followed via various roundabouts, always signed N120 Burgos, as far as Nájera. It you do not feel happy about riding along the N120, a shale track for walkers runs parallel to it, although it is hardly fair to the walkers, who do not need cyclists constantly forcing their way past. The N120 leads across hilly open country, with little in the way of remarkable or picturesque scenery except vineyards, before coming

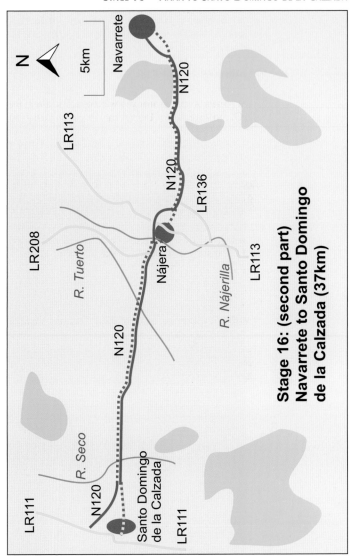

Stage 16: (second part)
Navarrete to Santo Domingo
de la Calzada (37km)

to the industrial outskirts of Nájera. Turn left here and descend through narrow streets until the bridge over the River Nájerilla is reached.

Nájera 485m (924/628)

Refuge (may be unsympathetic to cyclists), Hotel San Fernando (941 361138), Hostal Hispano (941 36 36 15). The Fonda El Moro, Calle de los Martires 21, has secure cycle storage but little else to recommend it. There is a campsite, shops including cycle repairs, banks, restaurants and bars.

Santo Domingo de la Calzada – pavement pilgrim

Nájera is an interesting old town backed by red sandstone cliffs. The Franciscan Monastery of Santa María la Real should not be missed, nor should the churches of San Miguel and Santa Cruz. The municipal swimming pool may give free access on production of a pilgrim passport. There is a pleasant shady park alongside the river, close to the swimming pool.

To leave Nájera ride back to the N120 and turn left onto it. The riding is easy, through rolling countryside often covered with the vines from which the famous local rioja wine is made. After about 17km a well-signed right slip is taken to cross the N120. This leads into the centre of

Santo Domingo de la Calzada 639m (944/608)

Refuge, Hospederia Santa Teresita (941 340700), hotels, Hostal del Rio (941 340277), rooms, restaurants, camp-site, banks, supermarket, shops, cycle repairs and bars.
The town is named after the man who spent his life caring for pilgrims and improving their lot. He is buried in the cathedral. Spend some time in the cathedral, with its hen-coop – the story behind it is a wonderful one – although you may be put out at having to pay to see two scraggy fowls in a church. The ancient pilgrim hospice is now a luxurious parador. The whole of the old part of the town with its narrow alleyways should not be missed.

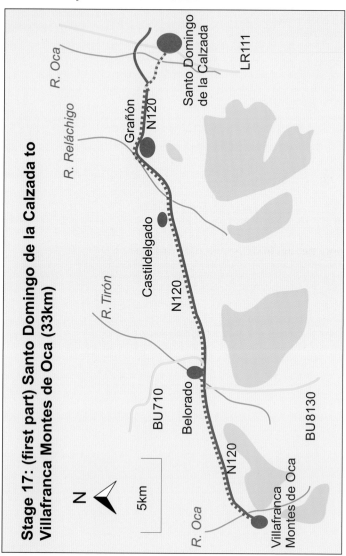

Stage 17: (first part) Santo Domingo de la Calzada to Villafranca Montes de Oca (33km)

N

5km

R. Oca

R. Reláchigo

Grañón

N120

Santo Domingo de la Calzada

LR111

Castildelgado

N120

R. Tirón

BU710

Belorado

N120

BU8130

R. Oca

Villafranca Montes de Oca

THE WAY OF ST JAMES – A CYCLISTS' GUIDE

STAGE 17
Santo Domingo de la Calzada to Burgos (70km)

Route	The whole of this stage is spent on the N120, but it is a hard ride. The Montes de Oca are hilly if not mountainous.
Surfaces	The road is wide with cycle lanes much of the way. The approach to Burgos can be very busy, but if you are fortunate enough to travel on a Sunday, you will find it devoid of traffic! Close to Belorado the surface is rough.
See	The rioja vineyards and beautiful scenery of the Montes de Oca. If time, the simple elegance of the church at San Juan de Ortega, and the magnificent buildings and boulevards which adorn Burgos.

Leave the town by the N120 heading for Burgos. This road is followed, with minor diversions, for the whole of the stage. The first 6km are almost level until to the left of the road is seen

Grañón 724m (950/602)
Excellent refuge which accepts bikes, and bars, shops and pharmacy.

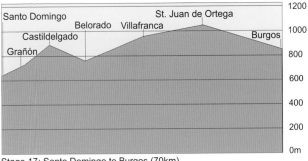

Stage 17: Santo Domingo to Burgos (70km)

This was once an important walled town with a castle, monasteries and a pilgrim hospital. It is worth seeking out the Basilica of Nuestra Señora de Carrasquedo.

The road now climbs steadily until it enters

Castildelgado 896m (956/596)
Hotel El Chocalatero (947 588063), bar, restaurant.

For the next 9km the scenery is pleasant, with woods appearing before a descent brings you to

Belorado 760m (965/587)
Two refuges, Hotel Belorado (947 580684), Hostal Ojarre (650 42 78 19), bars, restaurants and shops.
The outskirts of the town suffer from modern industrial blight, but it is worth seeing the churches of San Pedro and Santa Maria, which are used alternately, one in winter and one in summer.

The road surface hereabouts is heavily patched and uncomfortable to ride on. Once the River Tirón is crossed the woods appear, along with steep hills, until in 12km the road descends then climbs into

Villafranca Montes de Oca 948m (977/575)
A very basic refuge, Hostal El Pajaro (947 582029), Albergue San Anton Abad (947 58 21 49) and a bar, shop and pharmacy.
This mountain village is not very appealing unless you are too shattered to climb the huge hill out of it. There are the remains of a tiny, 14th-century pilgrim hospital, and the 18th-century parish church has a statue of Santiago.

The climb to the summit of the **Puerto de la Pedraja** (1150m) is only short – about 2km – but, therefore, steep with little shade. A kilometre beyond the summit the chapel of **Valdefuentes** appears on the right, with an excellent shady picnic stop opposite, with tables and seats made out of old kilometre stones.

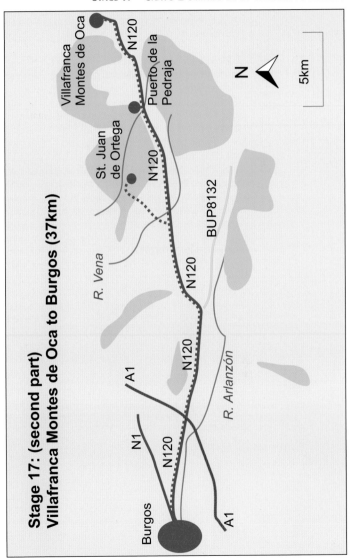

Stage 17: (second part)
Villafranca Montes de Oca to Burgos (37km)

A further 11km beyond this point a road to the right leads in 4km to

St Juan de Ortega 1040m (991/561)
Refuge (very basic – cold water and no heating), Albergue Monasterio (947 58 21 49), friendly bar and fountain.
See the beautiful pilgrim church of St Nicolás de Bari alongside the monastery where lie the earthly remains of Saint Juan, who made it his life's work to provide shelter for the weary pilgrims who passed that way.

Retrace your steps to the N120 and sweep downhill all the way into Burgos – this is one of the longest downhill stretches since leaving Le Puy. Follow the signs into the centre of Burgos. If you do not deviate the route is simple (ignore all motorway signs).

Burgos 856m (1014/538)
St Juan de Ortega – sarcophagus of St Nicolás de Bari

Burgos has a refuge in its park, Hotel Azofra (947 462003), Hostal San Juan (947 205134, which offers a pilgrim discount and secure cycle storage), Hostal La Tesorera (947 22 00 01), fondas, a campsite and tourist

134

Statue of El Cid

office, as well as a full range of shops including cycle repairs, supermarkets, a post office, bars, restaurants and banks.

Burgos, the financial capital of Spain, is a beautiful city with wide, tree-lined streets, a fascinating old quarter and a series of canals and rivers. One of the most effective ways to view the main sights of Burgos is from the 'Little Train', which offers a one-hour journey around the city at very little cost. The cathedral is breathtaking and should not be missed, both for its external architecture and its roof. Do not miss the Hospital del Rey, the great Arco de Santa Maria gateway, or the Casa del Cordón with its fantastic sculptured doorway.

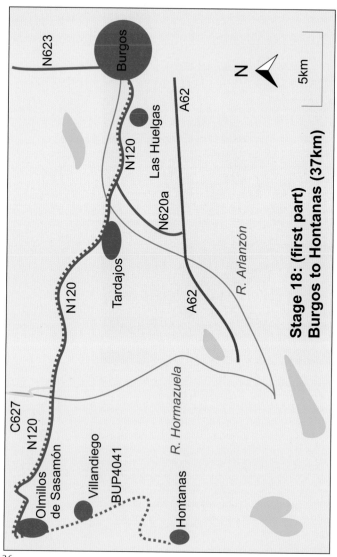

Stage 18: (first part)
Burgos to Hontanas (37km)

STAGE 18

Burgos to Frómista (73km)

Route	Straightforward as far as Argaño, but then complicated as far as Castrojeriz. After that the route is obvious and well signed.
Surfaces	Excellent except for the stretch between the far side of Argaño and Castrojeriz, which can be rough.
See	The incredible monastery at Las Huelgas, the many small villages of the Meseta, and the carvings on the Church of San Martín in Frómista.
Warning	This is the first of four days crossing the Meseta where the weather can be expected to be extreme. Ample food and drink should be taken and it should remembered that the water supply is often curtailed between 8.00am and 8.00pm in summer.

The N120 out of Burgos in a westerly direction is well signed to León and finding it should prove no problem – there is even a special cycle track. On the immediate outskirts of the city is to be found, clearly signed to the left of the N120, the Monastery of Las Huelgas (bars), which should not be missed, although it does not open

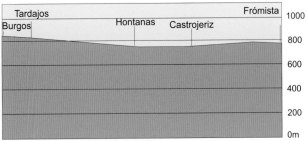

Stage 18: Burgos to Frómista (73km)

until 10.30 am. Having visited it, return to the N120 and soon you will reach the small town of

Tardajos 828m (1022/530)
Refuge, two fondas, restaurants, bar, pharmacy, bank and shops. This is the last real fuelling stop before Castrojeriz.

Along this road, at regular intervals, picnic spots under the trees have been constructed and are most welcome. In 10km the road crosses the River Hormazuela at

Villanueva de Argaño 890m (1029/523)
Two hostals, restaurant, bank and bread shop.

From here the road runs alongside a high escarpment to the right, a hunting ground for the eagles and vultures which may be seen wheeling overhead on the thermals. The ancient town of

Olmillos de Sasamón 850m (1038/514)
hotel, restaurant and bar,

appears to the left of the road in 9km. Slip right to cross the N120 into the town and follow signs for **Villandiego** on the BUP4041. Ride through this village going straight on at the crossroads. In another 5km turn right, signed Castellanos de Castro and

Hontanas 750m (1051/501)
Two refuges, bar, fountain, swimming pool and 14th-century church.

Leave the village by way of a well-surfaced, shady tree-lined road due west, passing through the fine archway and the refuge at the **Convent of San Antón** before arriving in

Castrojeriz 756m (1064/488)
Two refuges, Hostal El Mesón de Castrojeriz (947 37 86 10), Hostal Puerta del Monte (947 378647), Hotel La Posada (947 378610), rooms, bars, restaurant and

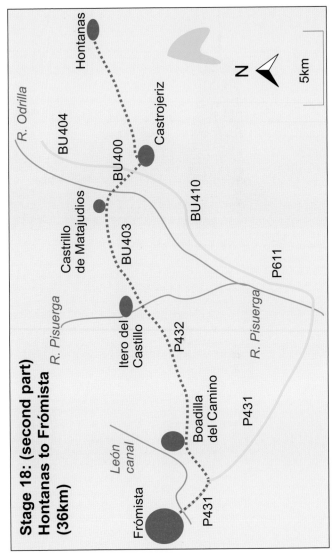

Stage 18: (second part)
Hontanas to Frómista
(36km)

Hontanas

Castrojeriz

R. Odrilla

BU404

BU400

Castrillo
de Matajudios

BU403

BU410

P611

Itero del
Castillo

P432

R. Pisuerga

R. Pisuerga

Boadilla
del Camino

P431

León
canal

Frómista

P431

N

5km

Castrojeriz – one of its three churches

campsite, bank, post office, shops, supermarket and pharmacy. Castrojeriz is not the most welcoming of places. The refuge wardens are unfriendly, categorically refusing cyclists, the shopkeepers are surly, and the post office does not carry stamps for outside Spain. There is, however, a genuine welcome at the Hostal el Mesón, where rooms are air-conditioned. However, the food here is at best ordinary.

The three churches of Nuestra Señora de la Manzana, San Juan and San Domingo are worth a visit, but there is an entrance fee. It is possible to climb up to the castle on the hill to enjoy a fine panorama.

Leave Castrojeriz in a northwesterly direction on the BU400, signed CAMINO. After 4km turn left at **Castrillo de Matajudios**, a village of brown adobe houses, onto the BU403, signed to Frómista. The road now heads out across the Meseta, passing close to abandoned villages whose ochre adobe walls blend with the bare soil. This road crosses a series of low ridges which means a series of short climbs and descents, but once the River Pisuerga is crossed, the road, now the P432, becomes almost level. Both sides of this road are covered in masses of wild flowers which add colour to what would otherwise be a drab landscape of uncultivated fields. A further 9km along this road will be found the village of

Boadilla del Camino 782m (1081/471)

Two refuges, one private albergue (979 810284), which accepts bikes, bar, restaurant, shops and fountain.

This fascinating place has a beautiful church with an exquisite carved font and an ancient pillory (rollo) in a tiny square outside.

It is quite common in this area to find local people walking along the roads rather than using any form of transport. After a further 3km turn right onto the P431 which, after crossing the canal close to a long staircase of gateless locks, brings you into

Boadilla del Camino – ancient rollo

Frómista 780m (1087/465)

Refuge, Hotel San Martin (979 810000), Hostal Telmo (979 811028), Pensión Marisa (979 810023), Hostal Camino de Santiago (979 81 02 82), restaurant, bars, bank and shops.

The chief feature of this little town is the 11th-century Church of San Martín, said to be one of the most perfect Romanesque churches ever built. Its golden stone is carved into hundreds of creatures decorating the gables of the church. There is an entrance fee, even for pilgrims. Two other churches should also be visited – that of Santa Maria del Castillo, with its great reredos, and the 15th-century Church of San Pedro. Both are breathtaking.

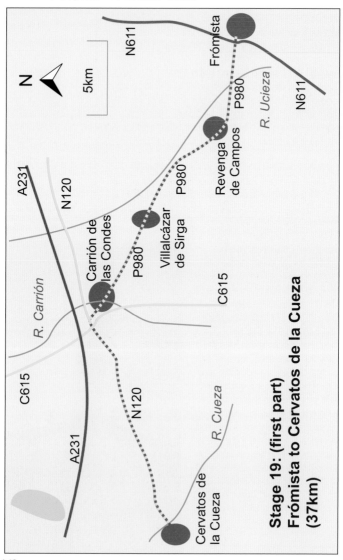

**Stage 19: (first part)
Frómista to Cervatos de la Cueza
(37km)**

STAGE 19
Frómista to Sahagún (67km)

Route	An easy ride, particularly after Carrión de las Condes.
Surfaces	Good all the way.
See	The museum at the Convento de Santas Clara in Carrión de las Condes, the Roman villa at Quintanilla and the ancient town of Sahagún.

From Frómista, follow the P980 west, quickly reaching

Población de Campos 790m (1090/462)
Refuge, shop and bars.
This is an ancient village with the remains of a pilgrim hospital and two 13th-century ermitas.

Picnic places still abound along this flat stretch of road with few bends. **Revenga de Campos** (bar, shop and Church of San Lorenzo) a further 4km along the road has nothing to distract the cyclist, nor has **Villarmentaro** (no facilities) 2km beyond. However, a stop should be made in the town of

Stage 19: Frómista to Sahagún (67km)

Revenga de Campos
– Jacabeo 2004

Villalcázar de Sirga 809m (1102/450)
Refuge, Hostal las Cántigas (979 88 80 27), restaurant, bar and shops.
Make sure you visit the Church of Santa María la Blanca, with its Chapel of Santiago and fine entrance portals, all in an excellent state of preservation.

After another 7km on the P980, the town of Carrión de las Condes is reached. Follow the road straight into the town centre, which is not obvious.

Carrión de las Condes 840m (1109/443)
Three refuges. The private one, the excellent Convento de Santa Clara with a fascinating museum and comfortable accommodation, recommends booking (979 88 08 37).

*Accommodation can also be found at Hostal La Corte
(979 880138), Hostal Santiago (927 881052), and Hotel
Real Monasterio San Zoilo (979 88 00 50). There are also
restaurants, bars, banks, supermarket, shops including
cycle repairs, and a campsite.*
Carrión de las Condes is a medieval town. The
churches of Santa Maria del Camino and of Santiago
and the Monastery of San Zoilo are very fine and
should be visited.

The exit from Carrión de las Condes is not easy to find.
Head north initially (follow signs for León and the camino,
N120), and when the N120 is met cross it in a westerly
direction and then join it at the next junction, signed
Sahagún and León. The road, which seems to stretch in
a straight line for many kilometres, is level and wide with
a good cycle track and picnic places at regular intervals.
  After 15km the road skirts the village of

Cervatos de la Cueza 844m (1124/428)
Bar, bank, drinking fountain and shop.

Keep to the N120, ignoring signs to Palencia. In 3km a
sign to the left indicates the remains of a Roman villa at

Quintanilla de la Cueza 840m (1126/426)
A kilometre of rough country road reaches a large building on the right which looks like an aircraft hangar. This
houses the restored remains of a Roman villa with extensive mosaic floors. It is beautifully set out with excellent viewing and photographic points. Open 1 April to
15 October, 10.00am–1.30pm and 4.30pm–8.00pm.
Having enjoyed this quite unique experience, return
along the country road to rejoin the N120.

From here to Sahagún the road is less level, although the
inclines are very gentle. There is a little more vegetation
than one might expect, but sources of food and drink are
very scarce.

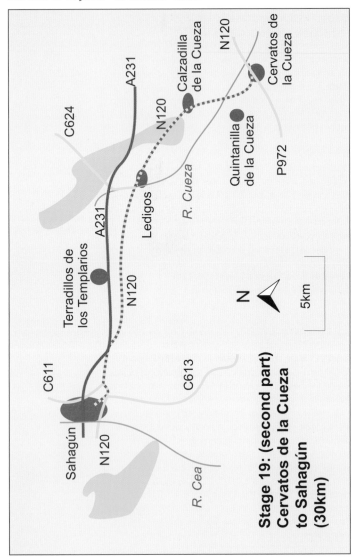

C624

A231

N120

Calzadilla
de la Cueza

N120

Cervatos de
la Cueza

Ledigos

A231

R. Cueza

Quintanilla
de la Cueza

P972

Terradillos de
los Templarios

N120

N

5km

C611

Sahagún

N120

C613

R. Cea

**Stage 19: (second part)
Cervatos de la Cueza
to Sahagún
(30km)**

*Quintanilla de la
Cueza – restoration of
Roman villa*

Calzadilla de la Cueza 874m (1133/419)
*Hostal Camino Real (979 883187), bar and shady picnic
place.*

Ledigos 863m (1141/411)
*Refuge, shop, bar and Church of Santiago stand alongside
the road.*

Terradillos de los Templarios 871m (1143/409)
*Refuge, bar, shop and 18th-century Church of San Pedro.
These villages are all along the way, but it may be difficult*

to buy supplies at any of them as the amenities often appear to be closed.

Continue on the N120 at the next major road junction. Picnic places can be found every few kilometres along this stretch. Traffic has now virtually disappeared on the N120 as it has all transferred to a new road which runs parallel – do not transfer onto this new road. Some 11km after Terradillos de los Templarios the road leads through the usual mixture of out-of-town light industry into Sahagún. At the junction, fork right for Sahagún. The road into the centre is clearly signed, and if followed will lead directly there.

Sahagún 863m (1154/398)

Refuge (987 780001), Hostal La Cordoniz (987 780276), Hostal Alfonso VI (987 781144), Hostal Don Pacho (987 780775), Pension la Asturiana (987 780073), campsite, shops, cycle repairs, supermarket, banks and bars. If you are intending to stay at the refuge, which welcomes cyclists and offers secure storage, head for the Church of the Trinity on the right soon after entering the town. The lower portion of this converted church is the tourist office and exhibition hall and the upper section houses the refuge.

Sahagún has an interesting old quarter near its centre with a number of churches and monasteries which should be visited, including San Tirso, San Lorenzo, La Peregrina and San Juan. A day could easily be spent here looking at all the ancient religious buildings spread out across the town.

STAGE 20
Sahagún to León (67km)

Route	Unless you have a real desire to follow the *camino* closely, the sensible route by bicycle from Sahagún to León is slightly longer than the walkers' route, but is smooth, quick and simple.
Surfaces	Using the above route, the surfaces are excellent as far as the outskirts of León, but here the edges of the roads are broken up by heavy traffic.
See	The attractive little town of Mansilla de las Mulas and all the great sights of León.
Warning	The traffic from the outskirts of León is dreadful and great care needs to be taken riding the last 5km of this stage.

Leave Sahagún by crossing the River Cea at traffic lights and following the road until it joins the N120, signed León (turn left and right at the edge of town). In about 6km, at **Calzada del Coto** (basic refuge, bar and two shops), the walkers' camino will be seen leaving to the right, but this should be ignored. Instead, stay on the N120. This wide, quiet stretch of road winds gently through several unremarkable villages with no facilities

Stage 20: Sahagún to León (67km)

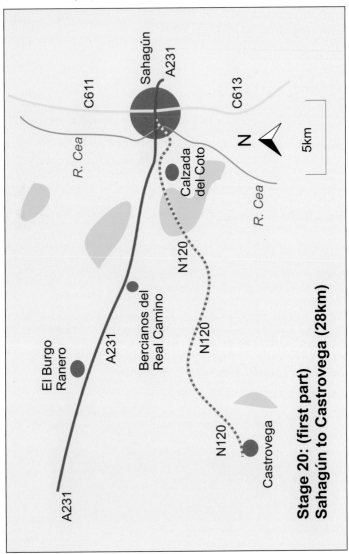

Sahagún

A231

C611

C613

5km

N

R. Cea

Calzada del Coto

R. Cea

N120

Bercianos del Real Camino

N120

El Burgo Ranero

A231

N120

Castrovega

A231

Stage 20: (first part)
Sahagún to Castrovega (28km)

Sahagún – one of many churches in the town

whatsoever until, after 28km, at **Castrovega**, a bar appears to be the only marker 1km before the T-junction with the N601.

Turn right here onto the N601, signed León, onto a much busier road with bars and hostals, usually accompanying petrol stations, at regular intervals. The cycle track is very wide and well surfaced. For the next 17km the walkers' routes via El Burgo Ranero join the road from the right, but cyclists should ignore them all, and having crossed the motorway and the railway line at **Valdearcos**, another 4km of easy riding will bring you to a left turn through light industry and modern developments into the centre of the pleasant town of

Mansilla de las Mulas 799m (1203/349)
Refuge, Hostal San Martin, Hostal Las Delicias (987 310075), rooms, campsite, restaurants, bars and shops and cycle repairs as well as a helpful tourist office (987 310138).
The town, with its 12th-century walls based on Roman originals, boasts an attractive 13th-century church and chapel dedicated to Santa María. If there is time, it is a place in which to linger and explore.

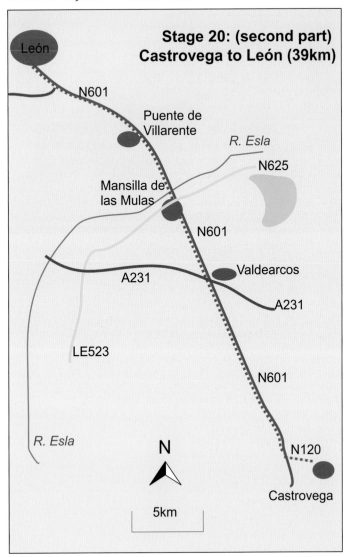

Stage 20: (second part)
Castrovega to León (39km)

León

N601

Puente de
Villarente

R. Esla

N625

Mansilla de
las Mulas

N601

A231

Valdearcos

A231

LE523

N601

R. Esla

N

N120

Castrovega

5km

Cross the River Esla as you leave Mansilla de las Mulas and continue along the N601, crossing a second river, the Porma, at

Puente de Villarente 774m (1209/343)
Hostal Montaña (987 312161) and Hostal Casablanca, bar, shops and restaurant.
The village's main claim to fame is its 20-arch bridge crossing the River Porma.

For the next 12km into León the road becomes extremely busy and the cycle track disappears. Both sides of the road are lined with industrial buildings, and the sooner you can pass through this cheerless landscape, the better. The road climbs steadily as it nears León, but the gradient is easy. Do not turn off this main road, but cycle directly into the centre of León. The traffic will be no busier than you have already encountered and the one-way system draws you inevitably into the heart of this interesting city.

León 822m (1221/331)
Two refuges, youth hostel, a large number of hotels, hostals, fondas, restaurants, bars, banks, post office, supermarkets and shops including cycle repairs. The Hostal Reina (987 20 52 12) has secure cycle storage and is very central.
León is full of fascinating places to visit. The tourist office, opposite the cathedral, will provide details of places to see, accommodation and a town plan. The cathedral with its fantastic stained glass, the Gaudi building which now serves as a bank, San Marcos which was once a pilgrim hospital and is now a parador, and the pantheon with its remarkable wall paintings and Romanesque church are essential viewing. If you really want to get a feel for the city, however, drop into one of the many small bars in the ancient quarter. It is easy to find – just follow the brass shells on the pavements.

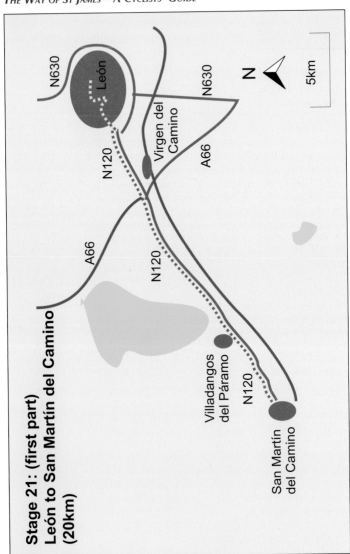

**Stage 21: (first part)
León to San Martín del Camino
(20km)**

STAGE 21

León to Astorga (44km)

Route	Almost all on the N120.
Surfaces	Good, except for a 'short cut' just before Astorga which is not recommended.
See	The statuary at Virgen del Camino, the church at Hospital de Orbigo and the cathedral and bishop's palace in Astorga.

To leave León, ride along the Gran Via Marcos, cross in front of San Marcos Parador, ride over the bridge and once more join the N120, following signs for Astorga. If in doubt, look for the yellow camino signs that lead out of the city. In less than a kilometre the ring road will appear from your left. Do not turn left onto it but continue heading west until, in 2km, you reach the suburb of

Virgen del Camino 905m (1224/328)

Hostal Julio César (987 30 20 44), Hostal Soto (987 802925), Hostal Central (987 302041), bars, restaurant and shops.

This village has a long history reaching back to the 11th century. The modern concrete church has unusual bronze

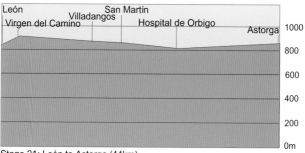

Stage 21: León to Astorga (44km)

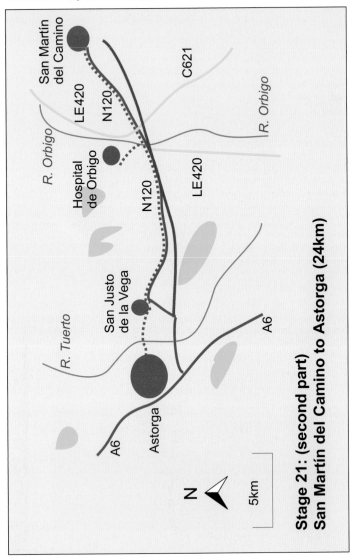

**Stage 21: (second part)
San Martín del Camino to Astorga (24km)**

statuary both inside and out, including Santiago pointing towards your goal. The people here are very welcoming.

Continue along the N120, avoiding the motorway (A66). There is a considerable amount of new road construction along this stretch and extra care needs to be taken. The road, for the first time in three days, becomes hilly, until it reaches

Villadangos del Páramo 890m (1236/316)
Refuge, Hostal Libertad (987 360640), campsite, bars, restaurant, pharmacy and shops.
Dating back to Roman times, this township has a church dedicated to Santiago, which has a painting of him, Matamoros, over the altar.

Some 5km beyond here the road skirts the village of

San Martín del Camino 875m (1241/311)
Refuge, shop and bars.

In another 6km a road to the right is signed to

Hospital de Orbigo – one of the oldest bridges in Spain

Hospital de Orbigo 819m (1250/302)

Two refuges, Hostal Suero de Quiñones (987 23 06 00), fondas, campsite, restaurants, bars, shops and pharmacy. The parish house, which is run as a refuge, will provide you with a stamp for your pilgrim passport, and offer you refreshment and a warm welcome even if you are not staying there. Sadly, walkers still take precedence over cyclists up to 8pm.

This town, whose streets are all cobbled, has an interesting church that is well worth visiting. One of the oldest bridges in Spain, with 20 arches stretching a total of 204m, provides access to the town for walkers and cyclists. This was once the site of a month-long jousting tournament. It is said that the victors rode on to Santiago where they presented a necklace of gold to the processional statue of Santiago Menor.

Astorga – Gaudi's bishop's palace

The road surface hereabouts is very poor and you are advised to retrace your steps to the N120, which has a beautifully smooth surface, and turn right onto it. Do

not accept 'helpful' suggestions to take a short cut and ride along rough tracks to Astorga. The next 15km into Astorga are across hilly terrain with little protection from sun or wind. Take a right turn on the N120 3km short of Astorga at

San Justo de la Vega 870m (1262/290)
Hostal Julie (987 617632), bar and shops.

Ride directly into the centre of

Astorga 869m (1265/287)
In the summer months accommodation can be scarce, with the three refuges, Hotel Gaudi (987 615654), Hostal Santa Ana, Pension Garcia (987 616046) and fondas full early in the day. Residencia Santa María de los Angeles (987 615800) offers pilgrim accommodation and secure bike storage, but is unmarked – take the street opposite the front of the cathedral and turn left into the first lane (San Javier, 17) – the residencia is through a doorway on the right. There are plenty of cheap restaurants and bars as well as shops, banks, post office, supermarkets and a cycle repair shop.

Astorga is a pleasant town of Roman origins with massive walls still standing. The cathedral and its museum are excellent and should not be missed, nor should Gaudi's bishop's palace, which is as splendid inside as it is out.

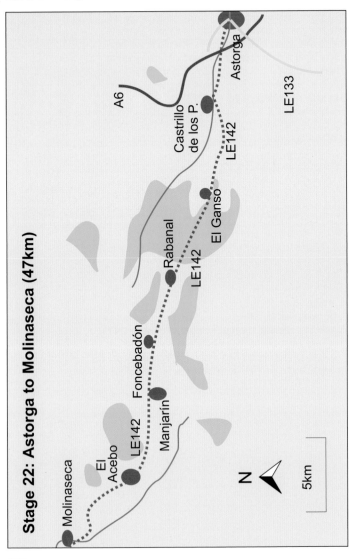

Stage 22: Astorga to Molinaseca (47km)

A6

Astorga

LE133

Castrillo de los P.

LE142

El Ganso

Rabanal

LE142

Foncebadón

Manjarín

LE142

El Acebo

Molinaseca

N

5km

STAGE 22
Astorga to Molinaseca (47km)

Route	A magnificent stage across the Montes de León. The route can be very isolated and exposed, so take plenty of supplies and wear warm clothing if necessary. This passes the highest point on the pilgrimage.
Surfaces	The roads hereabouts are not always well maintained and do suffer from severe weather. The concrete and cobbles in El Acebo can be lethal in the wet.
See	The stretch of the route as far as the summit at Cruz de Ferro is known as the Maragatería, with unusual Maragatos villages which are worth spending some time in. The mountain villages of Rabanal, Foncebadón and El Acebo are worth exploring, as is the country town of Molinaseca.
Warning	The route can be extremely exposed with little help at hand. The descent through El Acebo has claimed cyclists' lives, so take great care.

Leave Astorga past the front of the cathedral, along the Calle Porteria, and turn right at the end onto the Calle San

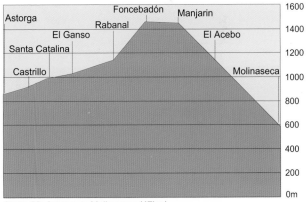

Stage 22: Astorga to Molinaseca (47km)

Pedro. Cross the A6 at traffic lights and follow the minor road opposite, signed for Santa Columba de Somoza and Castrillo de los Polvazares. This road is quiet, has a good surface, and within 1km crosses a bridge over the motorway. The first place of interest is

Castrillo de los Polvazares 910m (1269/283)
Rooms, shop and restaurants.
This perfectly preserved Maragatos village has heavily cobbled streets which are not conducive to cycling, but it is worth a visit. Look out for storks' nests on the chimneys.

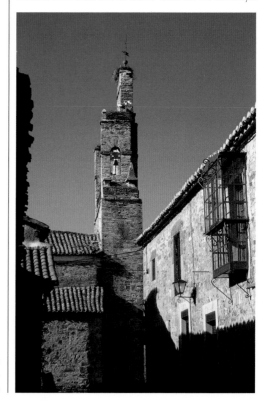

Castrillo de los Polvazares – Maragatos village

The inhabitants of this and 44 other villages hereabouts are known as Maragatos and used to be the muleteers of Spain. They have their own unique customs and lifestyle which set them apart as a proud race living among the Spaniards. No one knows their origin – they may have been Phoenicians or even Berbers.

Do not ride on through the village but return to the road (LE142) and begin a long steady climb, passing through a number of small Maragatos villages.

Santa Catalina de Somoza 997m (1272/280)
Refuge, bars and campsite.

El Ganso 1020m (1277/275)
Refuge (very basic) and two bars.
Visit the Church of Santiago, if only for shelter in bad weather.

The *camino* at this point takes the form of a shale track alongside the road with a convenient picnic spot alongside. 20km after leaving Astorga enter the hillside village of

Rabanal del Camino 1149m (1285/267)
Three refuges – the excellent English refuge is closed until 4.00pm, but the municipal refuges offer rest and refreshment all day for the weary pilgrim. Accommodation is also available at the Hostal el Refugio (987 63 15 92), which is not a refuge, the Posada de Gaspar (987 63 16 29), the Posada El Tesin (635 52 75 22) and at bars which offer rooms.
Surprisingly, this tiny village has three churches, all worth visiting, indicating its former importance as a staging post on the way to Santiago.

The climb over the Montes de León now begins in earnest on a well-surfaced road. It is very exposed in places and severe weather conditions, such as snow, hail, ice, gales and torrential rain, are commonplace throughout the year. If in doubt, take local advice before crossing these

Cruz de Ferro – almost the highest point on the pilgrimage

mountains. After 5km there appears to the left the once abandoned and now reoccupied village of

Foncebadón 1495m (1290/262)
Refuge, bar and Hotel El Convento (658 97 48 18).
The remains of 12th-century pilgrim buildings, including a church and a hospital, still exist, and life is gradually returning to this once abandoned village.

The road climbs on for another 3km to the **Cruz de Ferro** (1504m), which is erected on a huge pile of stones left by pilgrims to signify the unloading of their burden of sins. Do not assume that this mound marks the summit (1517m), however, although the views in all directions are quite stupendous. The summit is 3km further on, at an unmarked spot, and even then the road dips and climbs several times before reaching the refuge at the abandoned village of

Manjarín 1451m (1296/256)
Basic refuge. Coffee and support are offered to all pilgrims who hear the summoning bell of Tomás, the host.

From this point the road begins an ever-steepening descent to Molinaseca, passing on the way the fascinating mountain village of

El Acebo 1145m (1302/250)
Three refuges, rooms, bars and drinking fountain.
Like other mountain hamlets, El Acebo's main road runs through its centre, although the road is not smooth tarmac, but concrete and slippery cobbles with a gutter running down the centre. On bicycles this is a potential death trap

and extreme care should be taken, even in dry weather. If it is raining, get off and walk through the village – cyclists have died here!

Continue the long descent on the LE142. Soon a recently developed village,

Riego de Ambrós 840m (1306/246)

Albergue, Pension Riego de Ambrós (987 695188), Mesón Ruta Santiago (987 41 81 51), restaurant and bar,

is passed until the road crosses the River Meruelo in the pretty little township of

Molinaseca 595m (1312/240)

Refuges, Hostal el Palacio (987 453094) offers excellent accommodation, La Casa del Reloj (987 453124), Posada de Muriel (987 453201), restaurants, bars, shops, supermarket and pharmacy.

Molinaseca is an attractive village spanning the river by way of the Puente de Peregrinos. In the summertime the river is dammed at this point to provide a swimming pool.

Molinaseca – riverside Idyll

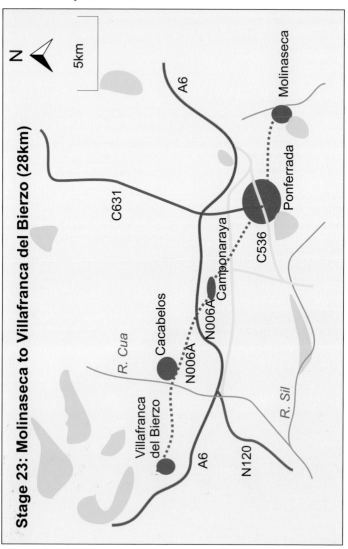

Stage 23: Molinaseca to Villafranca del Bierzo (28km)

N

5km

A6

C631

Molinaseca

Ponferrada

Camponaraya

C536

N006A

Cacabelos

N006A

R. Cua

R. Sil

Villafranca del Bierzo

A6

N120

STAGE 23
Molinaseca to Villafranca del Bierzo (28km)

Route	This is a very short stage, partly to provide a rest before the next stage's huge climb, but also to allow for getting lost several times, which is almost inevitable in the area around Ponferrada where signposts are scarce.
Surfaces	Reasonable, but difficult in and around the old quarter of Ponferrada where there are steps and cobbles.
See	The Knights' Templar castle in Ponferrada and the Puerta del Perdón church in Villafranca del Bierzo.
Warning	Map reading is very difficult in this area. Do not be too proud to ask the way in and out of Ponferrada.

From Molinaseca, continue along the LE142 until it reaches

Ponferrada 543m (1319/233)
Refuge, Hotel Madrid (987 411 550), Hostal Santa Cruz (987 428351), Hostal San Miguel (987 42 67 00), Pensión Mondelo (987 41 14 84) in old quarter, restaurants, bars, supermarket, shops including cycle repairs, post office and bank.

This industrial town is a very confusing place built on the side of a steep hill with mines and heavy industry abounding. Follow signs to the old part of the town, with its castle of the Knights Templar set to one side, go up another hill to

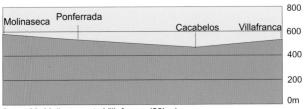

Stage 23: Molinaseca to Villafranca (28km)

Ponferrada – Templars' castle

the right, and it is here that the refuge and the pilgrim office to stamp your pilgrim passport can be found.

The exit from Ponferrada is even more confusing. Road numbers have been changed and a distinct lack of directional signs serves to complicate matters. If in doubt, ask for help, although locals often seem equally baffled. At the roundabout below the castle, turn third right and in 200m go straight over heading for 'Todas Direcciones' and the bus station. Turn left immediately before Carrefour Supermarket, signed Galicia and Madrid. Once in the suburb of Cuatrovientos, keep going straight on the N006A, pass under the A6 and in 8km arrive in

Cacabelos 483m (1332/220)
Refuge, Hostal Santa Maria (987 549588), hotels, rooms, restaurant, bars, shops and bank.
This busy, prosperous-looking town owes its wealth to the grapes and other fruit grown from its fertile soil. Try the El Bierzo wine, often drunk out of a saucer in this area.

At crossroads in the town centre ride straight on, and having crossed the River Cua, ignore roads to left and right and pedal into the hamlet of Pieros. Keep to this road straight through the village and as the road swings to the right, ignore any roads to the left until a junction to the right appears signed

Villafranca del Bierzo 511m (1340/212)

This attractive little town is the best place to stay before the long climb up to O Cebreiro. It has a famous welcoming, if rather basic, refuge (Ave Fenix, 987 542655), plus a municipal one, several hotels (expensive) including San Francisco (987 540465) and El Cruce (987 540185), rooms, Hostal Comercio (987 540008), Hospederia San Nicolas el Real (696 97 86 53), campsite, restaurants, bars, banks, supermarket, shops and cycle repairs.

Villafranca del Bierzo – Church of Puerta del Perdón

The Church of Santiago has the Puerta del Perdón, through which pilgrims who were too ill to continue could pass and claim the same benefits and indulgences as those who reached Santiago de Compostela. There are several interesting churches and monasteries, some fine old houses and a helpful tourist office. It is worth phoning the hostal at O Cebreiro from here to try to book accommodation if you intend to stay there at the end of the next leg. The tourist office will do this for you, using the telephone at the bar next door!

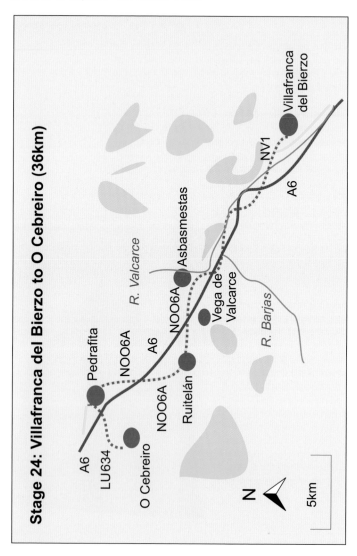

Stage 24: Villafranca del Bierzo to O Cebreiro (36km)

STAGE 24

Villafranca del Bierzo to O Cebreiro (36km)

Route	This is the longest climb on the whole pilgrimage, but because of this it is not excessively steep until the col at Pedrafita. In fact much of the journey is similar, physically, to a hard day's ride in the English Lake District. If the previous stage was managed with no hold-ups, arriving in Villafranca by 11.00am, it is perfectly possible to combine the two stages.
Surfaces	Generally good, but the old road can be subject to frost damage and may be rough in places.
See	Magnificent scenery throughout the stage. Examine the strange old houses in O Cebreiro and see the miraculous chalice in its church.
Warning	Weather in this area is very unpredictable, and you are advised to have plenty of warm and waterproof clothing available to wear at the summit, even in summer.

Leave Villafranca del Bierzo by riding through the main square and turning left to cross the first bridge. This is now the old NV1. Follow it to the second bridge but do

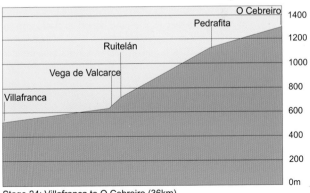

Stage 24: Villafranca to O Cebreiro (36km)

Travadelo – new and old roads

not cross it. Instead, turn right (camino sign) and follow the road until it joins the NV1 just beyond the road tunnel. Now turn right onto the NV1. After 6km pass through the edge of

Travadelo (sometimes spelt Trabadelo) 570m 1345/206
Hostal Nova Ruta (987 56 66 42), restaurant, bar and campsite.

After another 6km a road signed to **Ambasmestas** (all facilities) will appear. Take this. It is the N006A and from here it will take you on a delightful, quiet journey through mountain villages. Some 3km after leaving the NV1 you will reach

Vega de Valcarce 630m (1354/198)
Two refuges, Pension Fernández (987 543027), bar, pharmacy and shops.
High above the village to the left can be seen the Castillo de Sarracin, although it is too difficult to visit by bike.

Keep straight on the N006A, climbing all the time, and 2km later the road reaches

Ruitelán 710m (1356/196)
Refuge, bar including small shop and chapel to San Froilán.

A road to the left to La Faba should be ignored. Instead, watch in fascination as your road winds its way below the elevated section of the new road. It is hard to believe that the road above will be reached, but have no fear, it will! After a steady climb the road joins the new NV1 via a slip-road. Keep on this main road for a few hundred metres until **Pedrafita** (all facilities) appears. Turn left at the Pedrafita sign onto the LU634, signed O Cebreiro and Triacastela, a road which climbs steeply out of the village, bearing slightly right as it does so. This road is steep and unrelenting for 5km and can be very exposed and daunting in bad weather, which is often the case here. On reaching the O Cebreiro altitude sign of 1300m, turn left into the village of

O Cebreiro 1300m (1376/176)
Refuges, Hostal San Giraldo de Aurillac (982 36 71 25), Mesón Anton (982 15 13 36) and a bar/restaurant. Possible campsite in summer.
O Cebreiro is a unique village set high in the Cantabrian Mountains. It has only about a dozen houses, half of which are ancient pallozas (strange thatched buildings whose floors are below ground level, dating back to the Bronze Age). Do not miss the beautiful tiny church of Santa María and learn of its miracle.

Pedrafita Pass – views from the summit

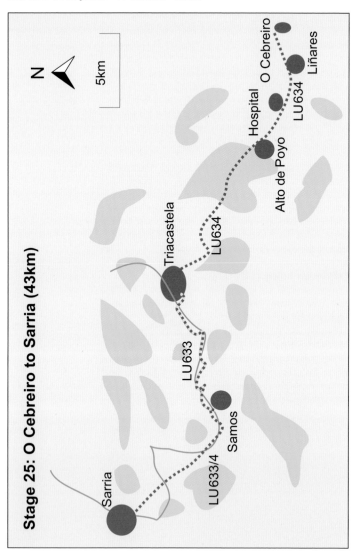

Stage 25: O Cebreiro to Sarria (43km)

STAGE 25

O Cebreiro to Sarria (43km)

Route	A pleasant if hard stage with some steep ascents and descents early on.
Surfaces	Recently resurfaced and generally good.
See	The fine Benedictine monastery in Samos.
Warning	The journey from O Cebreiro to Triacastela can be very exposed. Keep your rims cool on the long steep descent into Triacastela.

Leave O Cebreiro by the LU634. After 4km of undulating riding with steep inclines, the road reaches

Liñares 1260m (1380/172)
Shop, rooms and bar. This is a possible overnight halt if there is no room available at O Cebreiro.

Ignore the LU651 to the left a kilometre later, but continue to climb steadily for another 2km as far as

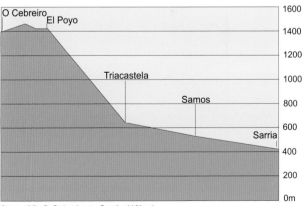

Stage 25: O Cebreiro to Sarria (43km)

O Cebreiro – palloza in the village

Hospital de la Condesa 1330m (1382/170)
Refuge which may be preferable if O Cebreiro is full, but it is not possible to purchase food here.

The road now climbs steeply in a series of three sharp ascents for another 2km until it reaches the high point of

Alto de Poyo 1337m (1384/168)
Hostal Santa Maria de Poyo (982 367167) and bar/café for a well-earned rest.
The weather along this stretch can be very severe, even in midsummer, and care should be taken in high wind, low cloud and driving rain, all of which can appear very suddenly.

From the summit the road descends slowly and then begins an exciting, steep descent of 12km. The road surface is excellent, with a large number of hairpin bends sweeping down the final 5km. It is advised that halts be made every few kilometres to allow your rims to cool after excessive braking. You will need no excuses to stop, though, as the views here are breathtaking.

Triacastela 665m (1396/156)
Two refuges, Mesón Vilasante (982 548116), Casa David (982 54 81 44), Hospedaje O'Novo (982 548105), bars, restaurants, bank, shops and supermarkets.
See the Romanesque Church of Santiago and the pilgrim hospice which was once also a pilgrim gaol!

The road, the LU634, signed Samos, climbs out of Triacastela for a short distance, then its number becomes LU633 before following a wooded river valley for 11km into the pleasant small town of

Samos 532m (1407/145)
Refuge, Hostal A Veiga (982 546052), Hostal Victoria, restaurants and bars, supermarkets.
The Benedictine monastery is worth a visit here – it also houses the refuge and has an extremely decorative stamp for your pilgrim passport. A visit to the cloisters will reveal wonderful frescos.

The road continues to wind its way in a series of climbs and swift descents through delightful wooded scenery, regularly changing its number between LU633 and LU634, until in 12km it reaches

Sarria 420m (1419/133)
This is a rather dreary town built chiefly along its main street. It has two refuges in the old town near the church of San Salvador up a stiff climb. It is possible to book in advance at the private refuge Albergue O Durminento (982 53 10 99). There are a couple of hostals, Hostal Londres (982 532456) and Hostal Roma (982 532211), and Hospedaje Mar del Plata (982 530724). You will find plenty of bars which serve food. There are also shops, supermarkets, post office and banks. A campsite is available near the river.

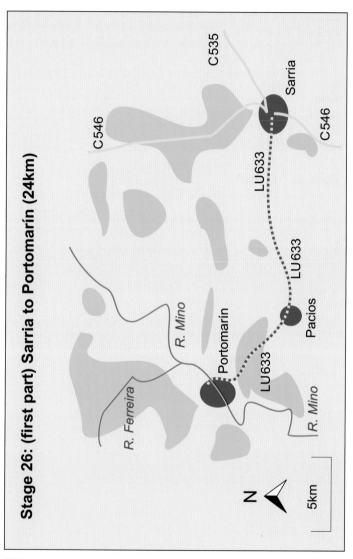

Stage 26: (first part) Sarria to Portomarín (24km)

STAGE 26
Sarria to Palas de Rei (60km)

Route	Although the high mountains have been left behind for good, this is probably the hardest day's riding of the whole pilgrimage and should not be taken lightly. There are long stretches with nowhere to rest and a number of long ascents.
Surfaces	Good as far as Portomarín, but extremely bad between Ventas de Naron and the N547.
See	The rather strange rebuilt town of Portomarín

Leave Sarria (left at the end of the town) on the C535, signed for Portomarín. This road soon becomes the LU633 and leaves by way of a very long steep hill. Having crested this, one is then faced with a series of short steep hills until, after 15km, the road reaches

Pacios (sometimes called Paradela) 806m (1434/118)
Bars, café, restaurant, shop, post office and bank.
The next 9km is one long sweeping descent which brings you, with many fine views, to the shores of a reservoir and the foot of the reconstructed town of

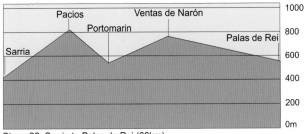

Stage 26: Sarria to Palas de Rei (60km)

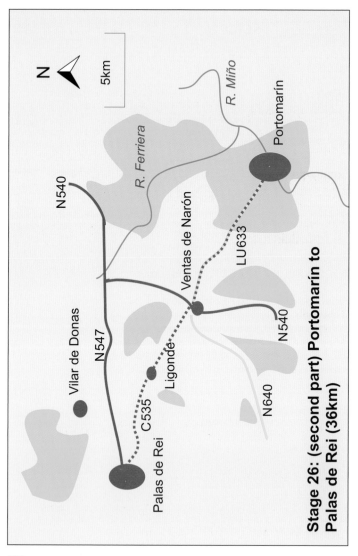

Stage 26: (second part) Portomarín to Palas de Rei (36km)

Portomarín – the flooded valley

Portomarín 550m (1443/109)

Refuge, Hostal Villa Jardin (982 545054), Pousada de Portomarin (982 54 52 00), Taberna Pérez (982 545040), rooms, campsite on outskirts of town, restaurant, bars, shops, banks and supermarket.

This town was moved, stone by stone, from its original site in the river valley to escape flooding when the reservoir was constructed. Its rather perfect layout seems strange, as does its massively fortified church, but a visit here is worth the very steep climb.

Exit the town down another steep hill before regaining the C535, which then becomes the LU633. A very long ascent with little shelter or shade follows until, in 13km, the N640 is met at

Ventas de Narón 765m (1456/96)

Bar and fountain.

This junction is complicated and it is essential you take the right road. Do not turn right onto the N640 (signed Lugo), but turn left and in 50m down the hill on the right (almost facing the refuge you can see from the bridge

Portomarín – the repositioned church

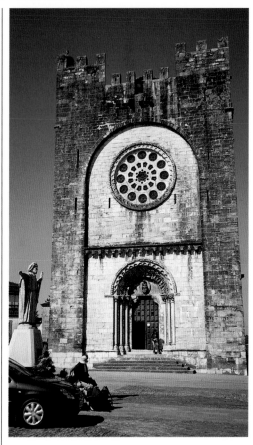

over the N640) take a road about 50m away, slightly to the right, signed Ventas. This is still the C535, leading across country through a number of tiny villages to your final destination for the day. The surface is the worst of the whole pilgrimage, with enormous potholes that could easily damage rims or rip tyres.

For the next 16km the road switchbacks over delightful countryside, passing through the hamlets of

Prebisca, Lameiros, Ligonde (refuge and kiosk selling sweets), **Eirexe** (refuge, telephone and bars), **Portos** (bar), **Lestido, Valos, Brea** and **Rosario**.

Wherever possible, follow signs for Palas de Rei. If in doubt, look for large bright-yellow arrows painted on buildings and walls. This road now meets the N547. If you wish, and have the strength to, visit

Vilar de Donas 602m (1476/76)
Romanesque church of El Salvador with fine wall paintings and effigies of the Knights of the Order of Santiago, a warlike body who saw their role as saviours of the country from the Moors,

turn right here and take a road to the left after 3km. If not, turn left and climb steadily until the road leads into the centre of

Palas de Rei 565m (1479/73)
This unpretentious town has a refuge, Hotel de la Plaza, Casa Curro, which serves some of the best (and cheapest) meals on the camino (982 380044), Hotel Casa Benilde (982 380717), Hospedaje Guntina (982 380080), fondas, restaurants and bars as well as shops, banks and a supermarket.

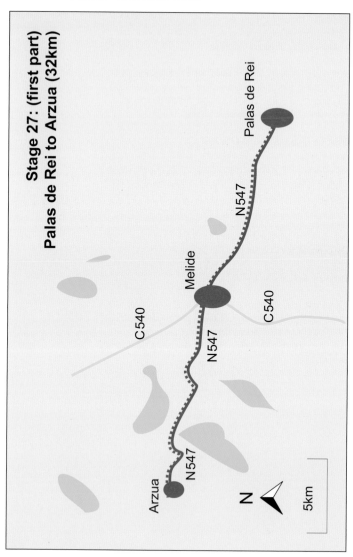

Stage 27: (first part)
Palas de Rei to Arzua (32km)

Palas de Rei

N547

Melide

C540

N547

C540

N547

Arzua

N

5km

STAGE 27
Palas de Rei to Santiago de Compostela (73km)

Route	Although the magnet of Santiago will be drawing you very strongly, it has to be said that while this road is well surfaced and has an excellent cycle track throughout its length, there are so many arduous hills on the route that you may feel an overnight stop at Monte del Gozo followed by an early morning ride into Santiago is more to your liking.
Surfaces	Good throughout.
See	Your ultimate goal, Santiago de Compostela.
Warning	The roads near to Santiago are complex and very busy. Do not be afraid to dismount and walk if necessary.

Descend on the beautifully surfaced main N547 (which you follow all day) which bisects Palas de Rei and ride through rolling countryside for 15km to

Melide 454m (1494/58)
Large refuge (981 505003), Hotel Carlos (981 507633), Fonda Xaneiro (981 505015), Fonda Xaneiro 11 (981 506140), restaurants, bars, shops, cycle repairs, supermarkets and bank.
This is a busy town, particularly on market days. It is worth visiting the Church of Sancti Spiritu with its pilgrim hospital for your sello, and the Church of San Pedro.

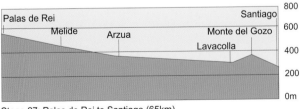

Stage 27: Palas de Rei to Santiago (65km)

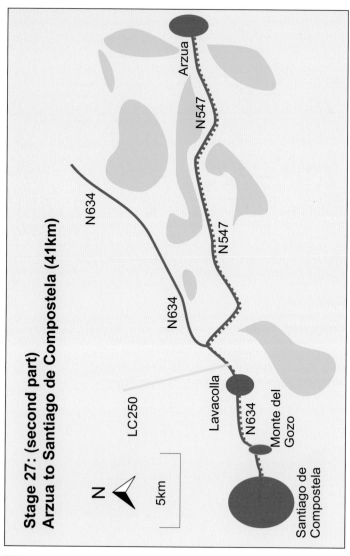

Stage 27: (second part)
Arzua to Santiago de Compostela (41km)

N

5km

N547

Arzua

N634

N547

N634

LC250

N634

Lavacolla

Monte del
Gozo

Santiago de
Compostela

From here to Santiago do not expect to encounter any flat roads. Each hill is about 2km long and the descents are of a similar length. After 17km of exhausting riding, the road enters

Palas de Rei – horreo, or grain store, found throughout Galicia

Arzua 389m (1511/41)
Refuge (981 500000), Casa Frade (981 500019), Hostal O'Retiro (981 500554), Hostal Rua (981 50 01 39) Hostal Teodora (981 500083), Hostal Suiza (981 50 09 08), rooms, restaurants, bars, campsite, shops and cycle repairs.

Arzua, famous for its cheese, has little to detain you, however, and Santiago is only another 35km away, or so the kilometre stones tell you.

The road now takes you through eucalyptus forests as it nears your destination. Bars along the side of the road become more frequent until, in about 18km, a motorway is reached with no entry for walkers or cyclists. Just before this, a road to the left, signed for walkers and cyclists, leads the pilgrim onto the old road, the N634, to the airport and the ancient settlement of

Lavacolla 300m (1542/10)

Hostal San Piao (981 88 82 05), Hostal la Concha, restaurants, bar and shops.

This was traditionally the place where pilgrims washed and made themselves presentable before entering the holy city. Nowadays the locals tend to ignore the pilgrims. Perhaps they always did!

Move on along the N634, which is quiet since the motorway opened, for another 6km to

Monte del Gozo 368m (1548/4)

Enormous holiday village/refuge (981 558942) developed to accommodate pilgrims for holy year 1993. Bars and restaurants.

The site of this huge refuge is clearly signed to the left, but it is unnecessary to visit it unless you are staying there as trees now obliterate the famous first view of Santiago Cathedral.

The road now plunges to cross the motorway. Keep straight on, always following signs for the town centre and the cathedral, or 'Centro Historico' (if in doubt, bear right, keeping the bus station on your left). It is possible to ride straight into the Obradoiro Square in front of the cathedral.

Santiago de Compostela 264m (1552/0)

The city has a large old quarter with plenty of reasonably priced accommodation. If one place is full, you will probably be advised to try another and may even be taken there. Try Hostal Libredon (981 576520). There are many restaurants and bars as well as a tourist office, post office, banks, shops, launderette, cycle repairs and supermarkets. Finally, if you fancy some truly unashamed luxury, the Hostal de los Reyes Católicos can offer accommodation unrivalled the world over – at a price to take your breath away more rapidly than all the sights of Santiago put together.

The new part of the city is like any other large Spanish conurbation, but the old quarter is worthy of several days' exploration. You should obtain your 'Compostela' from the pilgrim office on the corner of the Rua do Villar and the Rua Gelmirez.

You have arrived!

SANTIAGO DE COMPOSTELA

Many pilgrims leave Santiago feeling disappointed. They have travelled hundreds, sometimes thousands, of miles to find a city teeming with non-pilgrim tourists sporting broomstick staffs and plastic shells and gourds. What an anticlimax! But wait, there is more to this ancient city than that, although it may not easily reveal its true treasures.

Most certainly one cannot miss the cathedral, with its evocative sculptures, fine treasures, and awe-inspiring botafumeiro filling the sanctuary with holy incense, but this is the tourist's domain. Once the weary pilgrim has paid his respects to Saint James, he should decide to spend a few days in the city, teasing out its true beauty.

Santiago de Compostela – statue of St James in the cathedral

The best place to view the whole ancient quarter of Santiago is from the Carballera de Santa Susana, a leafy park that used to be a fairground, situated just beyond the Porta Faxeiras, where the old town meets the new. An afternoon strolling here gives a totally new insight into this cosmopolitan city.

Another quiet sanctuary is the cloister of Santiago's university alongside the Plaza del Obradoiro. This portion of the university usually houses exhibitions, so entrance to it is rarely a problem. Sit and reflect here and you will soon be transported back to a time when scholars from all over the world were drawn here to study and marvel at the city's fine buildings.

In contrast, the Church of San Martiño Pinario will overwhelm you with its Baroque architecture, both inside and out. Its interior, in particular, is so ornate as to stun the visitor into startled silence. Gilded cherubs dance exuberantly around blazing suns and the whole ensemble seems to have once adorned a fairground organ.

If you are looking for real life, however, head to the northwest of the city beyond the Puerta del Camino. Here you will discover the Convent of San Domingos de Bonaval. It is beyond the tourist zone and therefore rarely visited, yet it houses two wonders. The first is an incredible triple spiral staircase similar in design to that of da Vinci at Chambord in France. The second and greater wonder, however, is the enormous and beautifully displayed museum of Galician life. It would be easy to spend a whole day here wandering from gallery to gallery, savouring the true nature of this northwest corner of Spain.

If you would like somewhere to sit and watch the world go by, why not use one of the benches in the Praza de Fonseca. This is one of the few tree-lined squares in the old city. It has a tinkling fountain and is only a stone's throw from the bustling Praza do Obradoiro, where street traders ply their wares and tourists try to photograph everything.

APPENDIX 1

Santiago de Compostela
to Padrón (20km each way)

It is said that the boat that carried Saint James and his two followers was washed up on the shores of northwest Spain at a village called Iria Flavia, now known as Padrón, about 20km away from Santiago de Compostela. River silting has meant that Padrón is no longer on the coast, but is instead on the estuary of the River Ulla about 10km from a large inlet that leads to the Atlantic proper.

If you wish to make a short pilgrimage to this holy spot, it is only a couple of hours' ride (on a rather unpleasant road) to Padrón, which is itself quite a pretty little town.

Leave Santiago in a southwesterly direction on the N550, signed for Pontevedra. This is a busy road, initially lined with warehouses, light industry and all the paraphernalia that surrounds most European cities these days. Gradually this thins, but the ride never becomes truly rural.

The villages of **Milladoiro** and **Esclavitude** are cycled through before the road descends gently into

Padrón 110m
Hostal Jardin (981 810950), restaurant and bar.
Surprisingly there is little to inform the pilgrim that he has reached this important site. After the commercialism of Santiago this may come as a relief, although more information from the tourist office would be useful. Visit the place where the boat is said to have been tied and the church built over the spot where Saint James was brought ashore. Once again, more information about these places would be very useful.

The greatest amount of information to be found is about a beautiful, peaceful garden on the edge of the town close to the railway station where a well-known local poet, Rosalia de Castro, lived. It is certainly worth visiting this

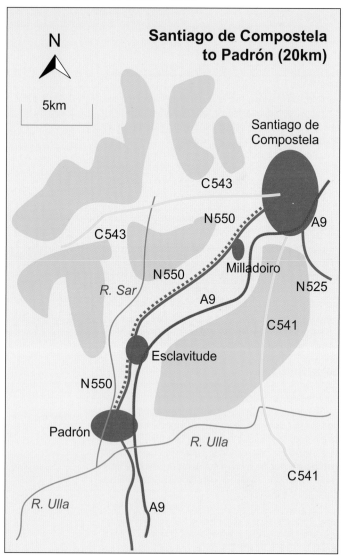

haven of tranquillity before facing the busy N550 which will lead you back to the bustle of Santiago.

Santiago de Compostela – floodlit cathedral

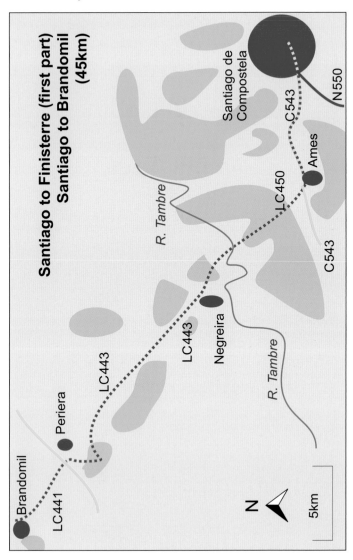

**Santiago to Finisterre (first part)
Santiago to Brandomil
(45km)**

Santiago de Compostela

N550

C543

Ames

LC450

C543

R. Tambre

Negreira

LC443

R. Tambre

LC443

Periera

Brandomil

LC441

N

5km

APPENDIX 2

Santiago de Compostela to Finisterre
(88km each way)

As far as the medieval pilgrim was concerned, Finisterre was the end of the known world, and having walked thousands of kilometres to Santiago de Compostela, most walked the extra few to visit this awe-inspiring place. Many modern pilgrims feel equally inspired.

By bicycle, at the same pace as the pilgrimage to Santiago, the fit cyclist can ride the 88km in a day then turn round and ride back the following day, but the discerning cyclist might decide to make this a three-day ride, staying on the coast near Finisterre to take in the beautiful coastline of northwest Spain.

Leave Santiago by riding downhill, past the railway station on your left, and follow the signs for Noia. This may entail changing lanes on a busy road, but there really is no alternative. Once the outskirts of the city are left behind, keep to the N543 for the next 11km, signed to Noia and Ames. When the centre of

Ames 240m
all facilities,

is reached, turn right onto the LC450, a well-surfaced quiet country road, and ride the 10km into the centre of

Negreira 350m
All facilities.

Look for signs to Pereira on the LC443. This is a good road with a cycle lane that undulates gently through unspoilt Galician countryside. After 17km you reach

Pereira 474m
all facilities
and the LC441 signed Baiñas is taken. Once again the

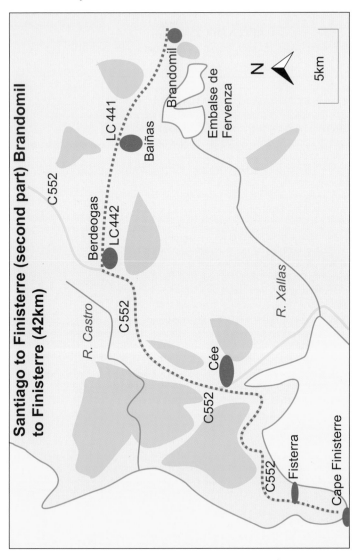

Santiago to Finisterre (second part) Brandomil to Finisterre (42km)

N

5km

Brandomil

Embalse de Fervenza

LC 441

Baíñas

C552

Berdeogas

LC442

C552

R. Castro

R. Xallas

Cée

C552

Fisterra

C552

Cape Finisterre

surface is good, yet the road is quiet, although very hilly in places. At Brandomil there is a beautiful picnic spot by a medieval bridge over the river and soon afterwards the road leads into

Bañas 492m
Supermarket, pharmacy, post office and bank.

Continue along the LC441 for another 5km until, at a T-junction, turn left onto the LC442 for 4km before reaching the hamlet of

Berdeogas 465m
No facilities.

Turn left here onto the C552 and ride the 13km through woodland to the busy little seaside town of

Cée 150m
All facilities.

The C552 is still followed as it climbs and descends steeply at times close to the coast before dropping into

Corcubion 95m
All facilities, including Hotel Horreo (the name for a grain store in Galicia, not something out of a Hitchcock movie!). Unfortunately, a large ugly factory belching flames and smoke does nothing to enhance this town's attraction.

Climb the steep hill out of Corcubion, still on the C552, and follow it for another 13km to the attractive fishing village of

Fisterra 75m
All facilities, including hotels, restaurants and bars. The English spelling of Fisterra is, of course, Finisterre.
The 'end of the world' is still another 3km beyond the town, up a long and tiring climb. The lighthouse marks

Finisterre – daisies along the way

the top of the cliffs where a restaurant and bar is available. Traditionally pilgrims have burned their boots here – or at least a T-shirt! Do not forget, however, that you have to return the 88km to Santiago by bike, so don't get too carried away!

APPENDIX 3

Full Kit List

Bicycle lights
Folding spare tyre
Water bottles
Cycle computer
Lightweight cycle locks
Cycling gloves
Helmets
Plastic tape
Tools
Spare spokes
Puncture repair outfit
Spare inner tubes
Bicycle pump
Velcro straps
Mini container of
    Swarfega

Dog-Dazer
Mini electric kettle and
    EU adapter
Mending kit
First-aid kit
Insect repellent
Army knife
Scissors
Lighter
Tissues
Polythene bags

Cutlery
Plates
Cups
Small plastic container
Dishcloth and scourer
Clothes pegs

Stretch washing line
Washing-up liquid
Clothes-washing liquid
Mini coolbag
Maps and compass
Guides
Dictionaries
Camera and film/spare
    battery/memory
    card (as required)
Mini binoculars
Dictaphone
Universal plug

Passport
E111 (entitles EU
    citizens to
    emergency
    medical treatment
    in EU countries)
Currency
Credit/debit cards
Pilgrim passport
Spectacles and
    sunglasses
Pen and pencil
Notebook
Prayer book (if
    required)

Toothbrush and
    toothpaste
Shower gel
Fibre towels
Toilet roll

High-factor suncream
Lip salve

Clothes
Thermals
Pertex jackets
Waterproofs
Padded shorts
Spare shoes
Coolmax socks
Compact sleeping bags

Food
Glucose tablets
Isostar sachets
Coffee/tea
Dried milk
Sugar cubes
Emergency meal

APPENDIX 4
Glossary of Terms

English	French	Spanish
an accident	**un accident**	*el accidente*
the bakery	**la boulangerie**	*la panadería*
a bicycle	**une bicyclette**	*la bicicleta*
a bottle	**une bouteille**	*la botella*
the bridge	**le pont**	*el puente*
a brake	**un frein**	*el freno*
broken	**s'éffondré**	*no funciona*
the cable	**le câble**	*el cable*
the castle	**le château**	*el castillo*
the chain	**la chaîne**	*la cadena*
the church	**l'église**	*la iglesia*
the city	**la cité**	*la ciudad*
the door	**la porte**	*la puerta*
the direction	**la direction**	*la dirección*
the field	**le champ**	*el campo*
the garage	**le garage**	*el garaje*
the gear	**la vitesse**	*el cambio*
the grease	**la graisse**	*el lubricante*
the handlebar	**le guidon**	*el manilla*
the helmet	**le casque**	*el casco*
the house	**le maison**	*la casa*
the main road	**la route**	*la carretera*
the map	**la carte**	*la mapa*
the motorway	**l'autoroute**	*autopista/autovia*
the nut	**l'écrou**	*la tuerca*
the oil	**la huile**	*el aceite*
the railway	**le chemin de fer**	*el ferrocarril*
the river	**la rivière**	*el rio*
the room	**la chambre**	*la habitación*
the pass	**le col**	*el puerto*
the pedal	**la pédale**	*el pedal*
the pilgrim	**le pèlerin**	*el peregrino*
the pump	**la pompe**	*la bomba*
the puncture	**la crevaison**	*el pinchazo*

the saddle	**la selle**	*el asiento*
the spanner	**la clé**	*la llave*
speed	**la vitesse**	*la velocidad*
the spoke	**le rayon**	*el rayo*
the square	**la place**	*la plaza/praza*
the street	**la rue**	*la rùa/calle*
the stamp (pilgrim)	**le tampon**	*el sello*
the (super)market	**le (super)marché**	*el (super)mercado*
the town hall	**l'hôtel de ville**	*el ayuntamiento*
the tyre	**le pneu**	*el neumático*
the way	**le chemin**	*el camino*
the wheel	**la roue**	*la rueda*

APPENDIX 5
Useful Addresses

There are many websites offering information about the French and Spanish sections of the route – you only have to type 'routes de Compostelle' or similar into a search engine. Many variants have also become available but we believe that we stayed as close as possible to the original pilgrimage route.

Confraternity of St James
27 Blackfriars Road
London SE1 8NY
Tel: 020 792 89988
csj.org.uk

Agence de Coopération Interrégionale et Réseau (ACIR)
Les Chemins de St Jacques de Compostelle
4 Rue Clémence Isaure
F 31000 Toulouse
France
Tel: 00 33 562 27 00 05
www.chemins-compostelle.com

Les Amis du Puy
(open 1 April to 15 Oct)
29 Rue Cardinal de Polignac
Le Puy 43000
Auvergne
France
Tel: 00 33 06 37 08 65 83

Cyclists' Touring Club (CTC)
Parklands
Railton Road
Guildford
Surrey GU2 9JX
Tel: 01483 238 337
cycling@ctc.org.uk
www.ctc.org.uk

Gîtes d'étapes
www.gites-refuges.com
comprehensive website and complete listing updated every year by Annick and Serge Mouraret and downloadable from the website

Los Amigos del Camino de Santiago
Apartado de Correos 20
Estella
Navarra
Spain
caminosantiago.org

European Bike Express
The Yard
3 Newfield Lane
South Cave
Hull HU15 2JW
Tel: 01430 422111
info@bike-express.co.uk
www.bike-express.co.uk

ALSA National Bus Company
Estación Bus
Santiago
alsa.es

Dog-Dazer
145a Northcote Road
London SW11 6PX
Tel: 0800 410 2888
enquiries@dazer.com

Cotswold Outdoor
PO Box 75
Malmesbury
SN16 9WQ
Tel: 0166 575 500
www.cotswoldoutdoor.com

Ortlieb Bags
Lyon Equipment
Rise Hill Mill
Dent
Sedbergh
Cumbria LA10 5QL
www.ortleib.co.uk

Trek USA
15 Old Bridge Way
Shefford
Bedfordshire SG17 5HQ
Tel: 01462 811458
www.trekbikes.com

APPENDIX 6
Bibliography

Hal Bishop *The Way of St James (The GR65)*, Cicerone Press, 1993
ISBN 978 1 85284 029 7 *Out of print*

Alison Raju *The Way of St James: Le Puy to the Pyrenees*, 2nd edn, Cicerone Press, 2012
ISBN 978 1 85284 608

Alison Raju *The Way of St James: Pyrenees–Santiago–Finisterre*, Cicerone Press, 2011
ISBN 978 1 85284 372 4

Alison Raju *Le Puy to the Pyrenees*, Confraternity of St James, 2004

William Bisset *Pilgrim Guide to Spain* (Camino Francés), published annually by the Confraternity of St James

Betina Selby *Pilgrim's Road*, Abacus Travel, 1995
ISBN 0 34910 594 4

Michael Jacobs *The Road to Santiago de Compostela*, Penguin Architecture (Viking), 1990
ISBN 0 14014 3149

Xavier Barral I Altet *Compostelle – Le Grand Chemin*, Découvertes Gallimard, 1993
ISBN 2 07053 2496

Paulo Coelho *The Pilgrimage*, Harper Collins, 1992
ISBN 0 06251 279 X

Edward Mullins *Pilgrimage to Santiago*, Secker & Warberg, 1974

Rob Neillands *The Road to Compostela*, Moorland Publishing Co, Ashbourne, 1985

Dr Elias Valiña Sampedro *The Pilgrimage Route to Santiago*, Roger Lascelles, 1993
ISBN 1 87281 526 X

Elias Valiña Sampedro *The Pilgrim's Guide to the Camino de Santiago*, Editorial Galaxia, 1992 ISBN 8 47154 794 5

Cees Nooteboom *Roads to Santiago*, Harvill,1997
ISBN 1 86046 162 X

James Hogarth (trans.) *The Pilgrim's Guide – A XIIc Guide for the Pilgrim to St James*, Confraternity of St James, 1992

Hubert de Torcy *Carnet de Route pour Compostelle*, Le Sarment Fayard, 1995
ISBN 2 86679 184 3

James Bentley *The Way of Saint James*, Pavilion Books, 1992
ISBN 1 5145 399 7

Julie Roux *Les Chemins de Saint-Jacques de Compostelle*, MSM, 1999
ISBN 2 911515 21 8

Jack Hitt *Off the Road*, Aurum Press, 1994
ISBN 1 85410 306 7

Jennifer Lash *On Pilgrimage*, Bloomsbury, 1998
ISBN 0 74753 6511

Stephen Platten *Pilgrims*, Fount (Harper Collins), 1996
ISBN 0 00 627 954 6

Robin Hanbury-Tenison *Spanish Pilgrimage – A Canter to St James,* Arrow, 1991
ISBN 0 09984 730 2

Nancy Louise Frey *Pilgrim Stories*, University of California, 1998
ISBN 0 5202 1751 9

Phil Cousineau *The Art of Pilgrimage*, Conari Press, 1998
ISBN 1 57324 080 X

CICERONE INTERNATIONAL GUIDES

For full information on
all our guides, books and
eBooks, visit our website:
www.cicerone.co.uk.

Walking – Trekking – Mountaineering – Climbing – Cycling

Over 40 years, Cicerone have built up an outstanding collection of over 300 guides, inspiring all sorts of amazing adventures.

Every guide comes from extensive exploration and research by our expert authors, all with a passion for their subjects. They are frequently praised, endorsed and used by clubs, instructors and outdoor organisations.

All our titles can now be bought as **e-books**, **ePubs** and **Kindle** files and we also have an online magazine – **Cicerone Extra** – with features to help cyclists, climbers, walkers and trekkers choose their next adventure, at home or abroad.

Our website shows any **new information** we've had in since a book was published. Please do let us know if you find anything has changed, so that we can publish the latest details. On our **website** you'll also find great ideas and lots of detailed information about what's inside every guide and you can buy **individual routes** from many of them online.

It's easy to keep in touch with what's going on at Cicerone by getting our monthly **free e-newsletter**, which is full of offers, competitions, up-to-date information and topical articles. You can subscribe on our home page and also follow us on **Facebook** and **Twitter** or dip into our **blog**.

Cicerone – the very best guides for exploring the world.

CICERONE

2 Police Square Milnthorpe Cumbria LA7 7PY
Tel: 015395 62069 info@cicerone.co.uk
www.cicerone.co.uk and **www.cicerone-extra.com**